"People say three-star cooking is safe, but it isn't.

It's the most dangerous thing I know."

GORDON RAMSAY

CHEF

PHOTOGRAPHS BY *Quentin Bacon*

QUADRILLE

CONTENTS

I'm often asked where my passion for cooking comes from. Where did the great adventure all begin, and what's propelled me to the position I'm in now? To tell the truth, I've often wondered the same thing myself. All I know is that the moment I walked into a professional kitchen as a pimply 17-year-old, proudly clutching my first set of knives, I knew I'd found my purpose in life. From that day onwards, my sole ambition was to win three stars, and nothing was going to stand in my way.

Some people argue that it was the lean times of my childhood, growing up on a council estate and surviving on powdered milk because there was nothing to pay the milkman, that ignited my lifelong obsession with food. I'll leave that to the amateur psychologists, but it was a few years later in France that I realised just how deep that passion was and everything really clicked into place. I had been working at Le Gavroche and Albert Roux had obviously seen something in me, so he sent me to work for Guy Savoy and then Joël Robuchon in Paris. For the first time I felt completely free. No interruptions, no emotional baggage from my parents, no obstruction from previous mentors, I was completely cut off. I wouldn't even contact home for fear of breaking my focus.

I'd work double, even triple shifts in the kitchens, and then as a waiter in my time off. I was desperate to learn everything I could about the French respect for ingredients, their desire to get everything absolutely right. I almost became more French than the French themselves.

I guess that's where the passion is – in making every element of a meal as perfect as it possibly can be. To misquote Bill Shankly, cooking isn't a matter of life and death, its more important than that. That's why once or twice a year I wake up in a cold sweat, panicking about losing my third star, but if it happens, I'll just work my bollocks off and win it back again.

What do they mean, those elusive stars that have come to symbolise the hopes and dreams of every aspiring chef; those badges of honour – years in the winning, moments in the losing – that dominate kitchen life from first thing in the morning until last thing at night? And what does it take to join the elite three-star chefs in the world's most exclusive club? Michelin issues no guidelines. There is no formula, no crib to tell restaurateurs what the team of anonymous inspectors is looking for.

The only intimation is that stars are awarded simply for what is on the plate. Inspectors are assessing the quality of ingredients, the skill in preparing them, the flair for combining flavours, the level of creativity and, above all, consistency.

In practice, a single stars rewards above-average cooking for the class of restaurant it is in, be it a relaxed restaurant or formal hotel dining room. A second star reflects greater refinement across the whole meal, more imagination in the kitchen and the use of higher quality ingredients, of *produit noble* as the French call it.

A third star is rarely awarded. Here Michelin is looking for something truly exceptional, a complete mastery of the whole gastronomic process – from leading and inspiring a team to delivering faultless cooking at every service, every day, every week. There is no room for error: the *amuse-bouche* that opens the meal must be as perfect as the *petits fours* that close it.

Few two-star chefs have it in them to make that final leap. To succeed, they must show remarkable originality, invention and the ability to adapt. They must also inject their own personality into their cuisine, and let their character come through. A three-star chef must provide the magic, passion and excitement that enables the diner to sense that anything is possible. And that is something Gordon Ramsay has always understood.

"In a three-star restaurant we expect cooking of the highest quality – for it to show flair, finesse and balance. But more than that, we expect the cook's personality to show through. And that's what Gordon Ramsay has always done. He is a supremely talented chef, able to inspire his team to produce exceptional cooking on a regular basis."

"Sensitivity, passion, strength – these are the words to define Gordon Ramsay, a man who has helped bring cooking to a point we could only dream of a few years ago. After reading this book, we will understand why eating well nourishes the soul."

"Running a restaurant is like putting on a live show every day –
but without a script."

The cast assembles at 7am every morning, five days a week, backstage in the kitchen of Royal Hospital Road. Silently and in total concentration, they rehearse their roles: preparing up to 15 sauces from stocks that have been bubbling away overnight; prepping the vegetables; filleting the fish;

par-cooking the risotto; or caramelising the tarte tatins to be finished off during service. This five-hour *mise-en-place* ahead of lunch is when 90 per cent of the work is done. Front of house Jean-Claude, Gordon's long-serving *maitre d*, casts a final eye over the dining room to make sure that every

glass, every piece of cutlery is in place. Soon the audience will take their seats and expect another flawless performance. Better than anyone, Gordon knows that running a restaurant is like putting on a show, a self-contained drama in three acts. People come to be fed, but they also come to be entertained.

The smile on arrival, the discreet service, the playfulness of a pineapple and chilli soup – all are calculated to bring that buzz of excitement. "It has to be dramatic because customers vote with their feet. If they aren't excited by the way they eat, they won't come back, simple as that."

AND SO THE SHOW BEGINS. As in any three-star restaurant, this is signalled by the arrival of the *amuse-bouches*, literally 'entertainments for the mouth'. Their gastronomic function is to get the tastebuds going, to tease the palate with the promise of the delights to follow. More than this, though, they help to put diners at their ease as they settle into their new surroundings, drawing their focus to the task in hand – to surrender to the unalloyed luxury that is a three-star meal.

PAN-FRIED SCALLOPS WITH A MILLEFEUILLE OF POTATO,
PARMESAN VELOUTÉ AND TRUFFLE SMARTIES

Now the kitchen moves into gear. A pre-starter is dispatched, again to heighten anticipation but also to win the chefs a little more time to prepare the first dish to be cooked to order. "You don't want to give guests time to get bored, or they'll start picking holes in the décor. Their starter should be on the table within 15 minutes of ordering, max."

MOSAIC OF FRUITS DE MER WITH SAFFRON POTATOES,
TOMATO CONSOMMÉ AND OSCIETRA CAVIAR

"We create new dishes by constantly evolving the old ones. Ideas can come at any time, but often it is during service when you're busy and all the creative juices are flowing. You'll be dressing a plate at the pass and think… What if I tweaked the sauce, or added such and such from this dish to that one? Four or five menus down the line, a dish could have changed so much you wouldn't recognise it from the original dish that was its inspiration."

"That said, there are some dishes we will never change. My ravioli of lobster, langoustine and salmon, served here with a lemongrass and chervil velouté, has become a classic. I don't see how it can be improved in any way. It shows great technique and skill, and customers have complained when we've tried to take it off the menu."

RAVIOLI OF LOBSTER, LANGOUSTINE AND SALMON WITH
A LEMONGRASS AND CHERVIL VELOUTÉ

"We serve lobster in all sorts of different ways, including at one time with a carpaccio of scallops. One day the weather was too bad in Scotland for the boats to go out, so we tried using some very thinly sliced octopus instead. It worked even better than the scallops and an instant classic was born. Sometimes it happens like that – your arm is forced and you end up improving a dish out of adversity."

SALAD OF LOBSTER WITH OCTOPUS CARPACCIO,
ROASTED WATERMELON, BABY SQUID
AND A SHELLFISH SAUCE

"The minute you send a dish you're not
100 per cent happy with, you might as well go home.
Game over."

Gordon, his head chef Simone and sous-chef Clare are gathered around the pass, tasting a salad of lobster, roasted watermelon and baby squid. Gordon isn't happy. "These calamari, they've been fried ten seconds too long," he says. The rings of battered squid look a perfect golden brown, but in Gordon's eyes they are an abomination. "How do I know that? Because they should melt in your mouth, but we're all still chewing on the bloody things now. They've got to be in, out, seasoned and gone."

Gordon says he's never sent a dish he wasn't entirely happy with, thinking never mind, we'll get it right next time. "If it wasn't perfect, it should never have left the kitchen."

SEARED LOIN OF TUNA WITH
POACHED VEAL FILLET, SPRING TRUFFLES
AND CAPER DRESSING

CARPACCIO OF TUNA AND SWORDFISH WITH A
MIXED HERB SALAD AND BROWN BUTTER DRESSING

"We have used a lot of red mullet over the years. Originally, we served the fish with a light soup made from the bones, then we started using the same stock to make a beautiful creamy risotto. From there we changed the rice to pearl barley, and that's how this dish was born."

FILLET OF RED MULLET
WITH COD, SPRING ONION AND PEARL BARLEY RISOTTO,
AND A SWEET AND SOUR PEPPER SAUCE

"The first question, always, is are we delivering on flavour?"

A chef's palate is his greatest asset. The art of tasting is the first lesson everyone in Gordon's kitchens must learn. Make the sauce, taste it, season it, taste it, finish it, taste it. Every morning, his head chefs will be brought a succession of dishes to test: the day's foams, mousses and creams from the pastry section; vinaigrettes and ballotines of foie gras from cold starters; and so on. Each and every one must be tasted and compared against a sensory memory bank of flavours.

But how do you sharpen a chef's palate? Can it be taught at all? Gordon regularly holds blindfolded tasting sessions, when the chefs try each other's dishes and try to identify the ingredients, but, as he admits, you can only take it so far.

"You can teach taste up to a certain level, but you can't perfect it. You can open the door, but you can't lead them through it. I can't impose my palate on others, but what I try to do is to teach my chefs confidence, to rely on their own senses. It's not a snob thing, it's not about being sophisticated – I've proved that, coming from my humble background. It's about identifying the key element of each and every dish and focusing in on it, to the exclusion of everything else."

BALLOTINE OF FOIS GRAS WITH LABEL ANGLAIS
CHICKEN, MARINATED SHIMEJI MUSHROOMS AND
A PORT VINAIGRETTE

PRESSED FOIE GRAS WITH SAUTERNES
AND CAMOMILE JELLY, SERVED WITH TRUFFLE BRIOCHE

FRICASSÉE OF SNAILS WITH SPINACH, BABY ARTICHOKES,
MUSHROOMS, PANCETTA AND JERUSALEM ARTICHOKE PURÉE

"The snails we use are beautifully plump and sweet and come from a farm in Dorset. I love that. This seems such a classically French dish and of course, in essence, it is, but we've brought it wholesale across the Channel."

"This was an interesting one. We did a classic steak tartare with a soft poached quail's eggs on top; a scallop tartare topped with a deep layer of caviar was also on the menu. At the time we were using Japanese Kobe beef, which was very rich, and I wondered what it would be like to have a spoonful of salty caviar with it, to cut the richness a bit. This strange-sounding combination worked even better than I had imagined. I have since learnt that the Japanese have been doing it for years, so great minds clearly think alike."

"Nothing beats the excitement when the first winter truffles come in – first the black ones from Perigord and then white truffles from Alba. We use summer truffles mainly for decoration."

GRIDDLED ASPARAGUS WITH SEL DE GUÉRANDE,
SERVED WITH A TOMATO VINAIGRETTE

SALAD OF ASPARAGUS, BABY ARTICHOKES AND PERIGORD TRUFFLES
WITH A CREAMY TRUFFLE DRESSING

"Every meal should be in harmony.

You must find that perfect balance."

A good meal is like a well-orchestrated piece of chamber music. It should consist of swells and lulls, of melodies and counterpoints. Just as the conductor draws the listener from the opening prelude to the grand finale, so the chef leads the diner irresistibly from starter to dessert. There is no point crushing the palate with a powerful starter only to follow it with a delicate fish course. It would be lost. Equally, the components of every dish must not compete with each other.

"I always think in terms of textures and flavours. I'd never team a harsh herb like rosemary with something delicate like scallops. It would be too powerful – better a soft herb such as chervil or tarragon. The downfall of many chefs is that they pick at their food but never eat it as a customer would. So they forget that they've got to maintain that magic – not just on the first mouthful, but across the whole dish. That's the hard bit, getting that balance on a plate."

BUTTERNUT SQUASH VELOUTÉ WITH SAUTÉED CEPS, PARMESAN CRISPS AND
MUSHROOM AND WHITE TRUFFLE TORTELLINI

As the components of a dish become ready, chefs will carry them to the pass, where the head chef assembles them on the plate and adds the finishing touches, perhaps a micro salad of slender pea shoots and leaves, or a dramatic parmesan crisp. Then a final inspection before it is whisked through to the dining room. "We never add anything just for the sake of ornament. Every garnish has to earn its place as an integral part of the dish."

CHILLED TOMATO CONSOMMÉ WITH ASPARAGUS, PEAS,
TOMATO CONCASSÉ AND BASIL

Not so long ago, the sommelier struck a terrifying figure as he stalked the dining room, silver tastevin dangling self-importantly from his neck. He (and it always was a he) would sneer at our ignorance and humiliate us into delving more expensively into the list. The modern sommelier, by contrast, as often a woman as a man, is far more approachable and less chauvinistic in his loyalty to France. The list at Royal Hospital Road, rightly acknowledged to be one of the most impressive in the world, draws its bins from all the regions of the world, from America to New Zealand, and yes, taking in a bit of France on the way. And the sommeliers are as happy to recommend a bottle for £30 as for £3,000.

"Restaurants shouldn't be stiff and formal. They should be fun – and part of that fun is in trying things you haven't had before. I always ask a sommelier for a recommendation when I go out. After all, they should know the list better than anyone else, and know the dishes they are matching the wine to."

MAIN COURSES ARE THE MORE STRAIGHTFORWARD DISHES in Gordon Ramsay's repertoire, where the principal ingredient is allowed to sing. It's not just to keep the number of flavours to a minimum, but for a very practical reason. A fillet of salmon will carry on cooking on the plate, a sliced loin of pork will grow cold and dry out, so that means working fast. You don't want to be messing around with fancy presentation. In fact, the simpler the better. "On to the plate, out to the dining room, job done."

LINE-CAUGHT TURBOT ROASTED ON THE BONE,
WITH A GARNISH OF STUFFED BABY PEPPERS AND SPRING VEGETABLES

PAN-ROASTED FILLET OF JOHN DORY
WITH CROMER CRAB, CRUSHED NEW POTATOES
AND A BASIL VINAIGRETTE

"I first served John Dory on a bed of crushed new potatoes flavoured with olives and tomatoes, and a chopped tomato vinaigrette. This dish is pretty much still the same, but with the addition of fresh Cromer crab to the potatoes and a fine basil purée to the dressing."

CHAR-GRILLED MONKFISH WITH CONFIT DUCK,
RED AND YELLOW PEPPERS,
AND A RED WINE SAUCE

"If you can't get the small things right,
what hope is there for the big stuff, like the cooking?"

Every morning, while those around them are preparing for the days' two services, the head chefs at Royal Hospital Road are brought a glass of freshly squeezed orange juice and a slice from every loaf of bread. It's not a late breakfast – just the first in a long line of tastings to make sure everything is as it should be. It isn't unusual to taste different oranges from several countries, or a blend of them, before the juice passes muster.

Gordon's empire may stretch over fourteen restaurants and four continents, he may have ten Michelin stars to his name, but like all successful people he has never lost sight of the small things on which his success is built. Be it the positioning of a wine glass, the seasoning of the bread, the colour of a Bloody Mary – he knows that it is by such details that he will be judged. "You have to get those right. They set the tone for the rest of the evening."

"This halibut dish started life with a pink grapefruit vinaigrette, the tartness of which offset the sweetness of the fish. The grapefruit changed to orange and then to passion fruit, which we are still using, as its perfumed tartness is perfect with halibut."

HALIBUT FILLETS LARDED WITH SMOKED SALMON,
SERVED WITH CANDIED LEMON, BRAISED VEGETABLES
AND SMOKED HORSERADISH VELOUTÉ

PAN-FRIED SEA BASS WITH ROASTED BABY ARTICHOKES,
BORLOTTI BEANS AND A CEP VELOUTÉ

"Cooking fish is one of the biggest tests of any chef. It needs a deft touch and is much less forgiving than a piece of meat. Timing is all. To serve a stunning fillet of sea bass or line-caught turbot roasted on the bone is an act of such simplicity, yet it requires total confidence in your technique and in your raw ingredients. There's nowhere to hide with fish."

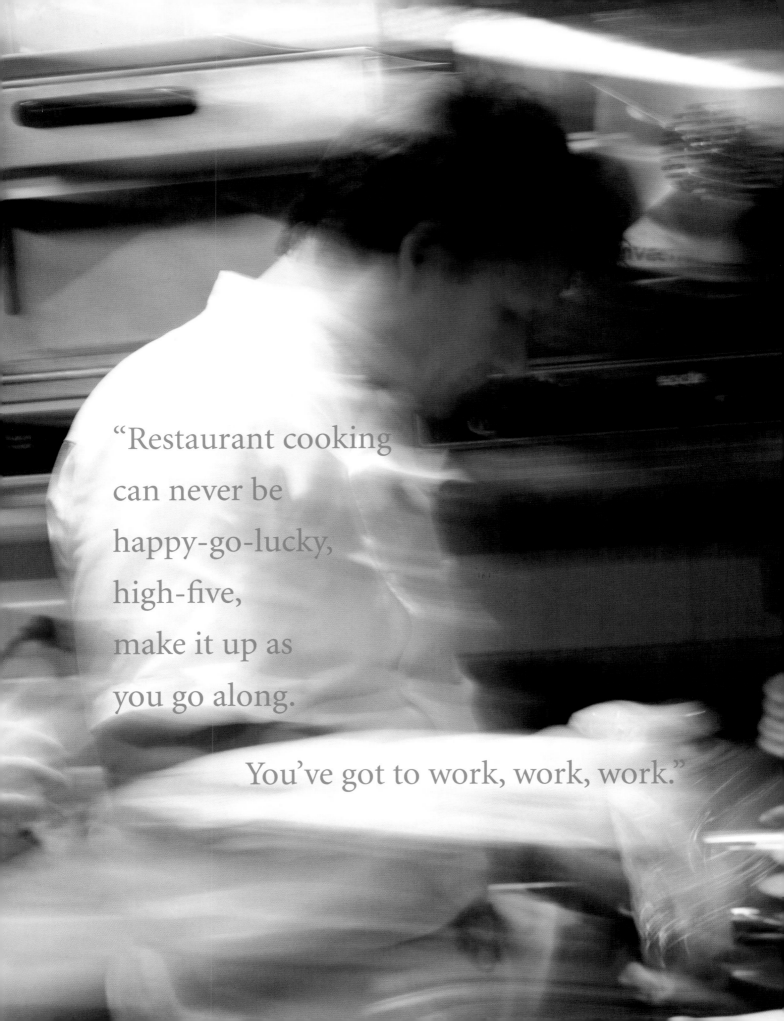

"Restaurant cooking
can never be
happy-go-lucky,
high-five,
make it up as
you go along.

You've got to work, work, work."

There's a common misconception that cooking is an art: all visionary genius and leaps of creative faith. In the best chefs, that certainly plays a part – the ability to conjure up an epoch-defining dish must come from within – but at its heart, cooking is a craft, one learnt through repetition and adherence to an established set of culinary principles. It's only once these have been fully understood and mastered that a chef can move on to a higher plane. In other words, there's no substitute for graft.

And no one can complain that Gordon hasn't put in the hard work. He has paid his dues under some of the most talented chefs in Europe, from Marco Pierre White and Michel Roux to Guy Savoy and Joël Robuchon, often taking a cut in pay and status in order to complete his training. When he left Le Gavroche in London for Restaurant Guy Savoy in Paris, for example, he went from head chef to kitchen porter effectively, only to work his way up again.

His reward now is that there's not a job he will ask one of his chefs to do that he cannot do better, be it boning a pig's trotter, filleting a turbot or making a classic beurre blanc. "I was determined never to be fazed or intimidated by an ingredient, to stand in front of it and not know exactly what to do with it. At Guy Savoy I used to watch the others peel ceps and then dry out the peelings to make cep powder, which would crop up in a risotto three weeks later. They never told me what they were doing, I had to work it out myself."

"When making a capon bouillon, they'd start by filtering the water through muslin, and the second it started simmering, they would ladle off the scum every 2 minutes for hours on end. I didn't understand why at first, but 8 hours later they ended up with a stock so crystal clear there was no need to clarify it. You can't help but see something like that and pick up on the brilliance of it."

OVEN-ROASTED BRESSE PIGEON WRAPPED IN PARMA HAM
WITH FOIE GRAS, CREAMED MUSHROOMS AND A DATE SAUCE

ROAST GRESSINGHAM DUCK BREAST WITH HONEY GLAZED BABY ONIONS
AND SALSIFY, MINTED PEAS AND A MADEIRA SAUCE

ROASTED SADDLE AND LEG OF RABBIT ON CAULIFLOWER,
HARICOT BEANS AND BABY GEM LETTUCE, WITH A RED WINE SAUCE

"You don't get to run a three-star kitchen by sitting

If Harvey's, where Gordon Ramsay trained under Marco Pierre White for 2 years, was known as the SAS of kitchens, a spell in his own has been compared to a tour of duty in Vietnam. The days are long – starting at 7am and often not finishing until 1am – and the casualty rate is high. One in two new recruits don't last the month.

"It's a hard environment, I don't make any excuse for that. It's hot, it's high pressure, and you've got to be physically and mentally fit. But that's kitchens for you: there's no room for fat chefs any more, and if you don't put in the hours, you'll never learn."

on your backside 16 hours a day."

NAVARIN OF LAMB WITH BUTTERED VEGETABLES,
CELERIAC PURÉE AND THYME JUS

"This dish – featuring two cuts of lamb – is always on my menu, even if the garnish changes regularly. The combination of the 'posh cut' of best end and the 'cheap cut' of shoulder is fantastic. We cook the shoulder very slowly for several hours, then pick the meat off the bone and remove any sinew. Then we press it, cut out rounds and pan-fry them until crisp on the outside and soft in the middle. It may be the cheaper cut, but the result is phenomenal."

BEST END OF LAMB WITH CONFIT SHOULDER, PROVENÇALE VEGETABLES,
SPINACH AND BASIL LAMB JUS

"Every fillet of beef, every saddle of hare, every basket of truffles

is a fight you have to win. You're up against yourself every time."

A box of artichokes has arrived at Royal Hospital Road for that day's lunch special: a salad of baby artichokes with asparagus and fresh truffles. A commis is peeling them by hand. In a lazy kitchen, they'd be dowsed in white wine vinegar to stop them going brown, but no such shortcuts here. Instead the commis' fingers work faster and faster, racing against time before the artichokes start to oxidise. That's the level of self-discipline needed in a three-star kitchen, where every ingredient must be treated the best way possible.

"At Guy Savoy, I learnt to handle every ingredient like a piece of precious jewellery. He would have me blowing the grit out of hundreds of morels with a hairdryer like I was Vidal Sassoon, but to see them later served up sautéed on top of a white truffle risotto was mind-blowing. Each one of them blow-dried to perfection – all that work for a single moment of pleasure. That's how I learnt to respect every single ingredient, to see it for all its potential and make it as perfect as it can be."

Roasted fillet of beef with a truffle and
root vegetable infusion

"The more confident a chef,
            the less he needs to hide."

Ask Gordon his favourite dish and the answer is the same every time. Not the tagliatelle of oysters and caviar he learnt at Harvey's; not his own slow-braised pork belly with creamed celeriac and Madeira sauce; but something he ate nearly 20 years ago in a simple restaurant in the Pyrenees – breast of lamb with roasted apricots and boulangère potatoes. "And that was it, just three things on the plate. It wasn't pretty, there were no frills, but with all the will in the world, no one could have made it better."

It typifies what he tries to achieve in his own cooking. Yes, there's lobster, caviar, foie gras and truffles aplenty at Royal Hospital Road, but you'll find no symphonies of this nestling in beds of that, just four or five clean flavours on a plate. "I'm always pulling back from adding more elements to a dish, always asking, 'Can I make this simpler?' Young chefs who lack confidence use frills and decoration as a security blanket, to mask the lack of focus on flavour. They think that if it looks good, it will taste good. But that's the wrong

message. I always tell them to take a third off the plate and start again." It's a mistake he made himself in the early days of Aubergine, "Because of the insecurity you feel when you're starting out". There were some dishes that were so over-complicated that only he could finish them off. He'd have his brigade prep the carrots this way, the leeks that way, and at midday they still had no idea how the dishes would be put together. "Sure, it was exciting, but that's no way to run a kitchen. You couldn't do that in a three-star kitchen."

"Slow-braised pork belly is a cut that will never leave my menus. It's so versatile that I've changed this dish around too many ways to number. We've served it with squid, with lobster, with langoustines, even with deep-fried quail's eggs. It's one of my favourites and has been with me since the very beginning."

PORK CHEEKS WITH PORK FILLET WRAPPED IN PARMA HAM,
BLACK PUDDING, BABY TURNIPS AND SAUTÉED MORELS

Veal osso bucco with boulangère potatoes, savoy cabbage,
turnip purée and its own braising jus

"Our risottos and the way we flavour and finish them has changed dramatically over the years. Fresh ceps are a dream to use, but very expensive. A sprinkling of cep powder – made by drying out the peelings in a low oven and pulverising them – is a great way to finish a cep risotto. We used to enrich this risotto with whipped cream but it made the whole thing too creamy, so now we just use butter, a little mascarpone and parmesan. It's the way the Italians do it, and you can't argue with that."

"There are people who think that Gordon has been lucky, but I'm not one of them. Determination, skill, bloody mindedness and hard work – these are the reasons for his success... this is his luck."

THE ONLY EXCEPTION TO THE MANTRA OF SIMPLIFICATION IS WITH DESSERTS. "That's the grand finale, that's the payoff, where you can stare at a perfect caramelised pear tatin or a beautifully presented bitter chocolate mousse with coffee granita for several minutes and think... wow!"

CARAMELISED PEAR TATIN WITH GORGONZOLA ICE CREAM AND WALNUT CREAM

"How can you improve on perfection?

Well, I'll have a bloody good try."

CARAMELISED APPLE TARTE TATIN WITH VANILLA ICE CREAM

"The tarte tatin is a classic. Whether we do it with apples or pears, plums or clementines, the principles are the same. Where we try to improve on this near perfect dish is by flavouring the caramel – with rosemary, cinnamon or star anise, for example. Cardamom is a brilliant spicy addition and walnuts give a great taste too."

CARROT AND WHITE CHOCOLATE FONDANT WITH DARK CHOCOLATE SORBET

TOFFEE SOUFFLÉ WITH BANANA AND LIME ICE CREAM

LEMON MERINGUE WITH MARINATED STRAWBERRIES

PLUM CRUMBLE TART WITH ALMOND FRANGIPANE

A menu can never stand still. Diners want to be enticed into trying new things, to share the excitement coming from the kitchen, so a chef must reinvent or die. But at this level, innovation brings its own risks and the stakes are high. At any time, three-quarters of the menu at Royal Hospital Road comprises tried and tested 'classics'; the rest are new dishes, which may in turn become regular fixtures.

RASPBERRY COMPOTE WITH TARRAGON CREAM

MARINATED PINEAPPLE RAVIOLI WITH MANGO, BERRIES
AND MINT SORBET

PINEAPPLE AND CHILLI SOUP
WITH FROMAGE FRAIS FOAM

In the old days, cooks were far more restrictive in the roles they took. They trained as sauce chefs, pastry chefs, fish and meat chefs – and there they stayed. Gordon has always been determined that his kitchen would be different, that his chefs should have an understanding of all the different sections. One result is a greater cross-fertilisation of ideas. The pastry (or dessert) section is a good example. "Ten years ago, who would have thought we would now be adding salt to a caramel; basil or bay leaves to a crème anglaise; or chilli to an ice cream?" He has taken desserts on to a whole new level.

SABLÉ BRETON WITH RASPBERRIES, VANILLA CREAM
AND VANILLA ICE CREAM

TIRAMISU WITH COFFEE GRANITA

APPLE PARFAIT WITH HONEYCOMB, BITTER CHOCOLATE AND CHAMPAGNE FOAM

"Pastry has always been the most creative
section, the one where chefs can let their
imaginations really run wild."

Raspberry, lemon and basil millefeuille with milk ice cream

Often separated from the hubbub of the main kitchen, the pastry chefs can patiently tease out their creations in relative solitude. The mornings are spent preparing their mousses and creams, their granitas and ice creams, their tuiles and cakes, leaving them a luxury during service denied to their colleagues – that of time. You can't hurry artistry like this.

PALET D'OR WITH CHOCOLATE AND HAZELNUT ICE CREAM
AND PASSION FRUIT CRÈME

SLOW-BAKED QUINCE WITH CRÈME CATALAN, PEDRO XIMENEZ GELÉE
AND ACACIA HONEY GRANITA

"A classic of mine since my Aubergine days, this is basically

a small taster of the desserts on the menu and is served for two.

The line-up changes regularly, but we often finish with our own miniature soufflés."

"Cubes, waves, pyramids, cylinders – chocolate is the perfect foil for the pastry chef's dark art."

CHOCOLATE PARFAIT WITH PASSION FRUIT
AND GUAVA COULIS

BITTER CHOCOLATE MOUSSE WITH COFFEE GRANITA AND LIGHT GINGER CREAM

"Cheese is another area where we used to bow to the French, but British cheeses are so good now they make up nearly half our board."

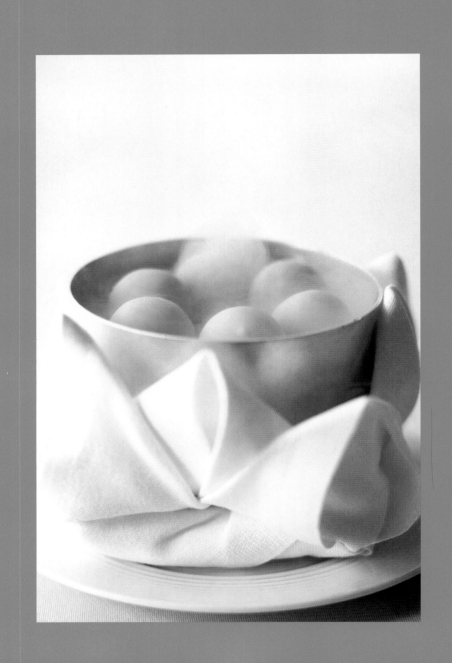

THE ARRIVAL OF THE PETITS FOURS SIGNALS THE END OF THE 3-STAR EXPERIENCE.

The curtain is about to go down on another bravura performance. This is the final chance to linger, to have one last taste as a reminder of the brilliance that has preceded it. And then it's all over, the last mouthful as extravagantly exquisite as the first.

"Whatever
happens during
a tough service,
every mistake stays
in the kitchen."

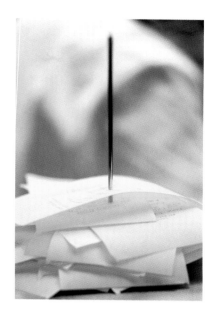

12.30am. Another day comes to an end. As the last customers make their way home, there are supplies to be ordered; fridges to be cleaned; floors to scrub; stoves to be polished "until you can see your own reflection, because that's the first thing that greets you when you start your day". It's also the time when the kitchen becomes the dressing room, a place for post-match reflection and analysis. Talk turns to what went right, what went wrong, "how when I said four minutes on the hot plate, it was four and a half".

It's also a time for bonding as chefs, waiters, porters – everyone – comes down from the adrenaline rush of a busy service. It's a close-knit team. Because Royal Hospital Road is open only Monday to Friday, the chefs work every shift and many have been with Gordon for more than ten years. They spend more time with each other than they do with their families. Whatever hard words might have been said in the heat of battle, all now is put behind them.

"Then it's lights off, bang. Ready to do it all again the next day."

"Gordon is one of the few chefs in possession of all God's gifts. He's driven, hugely talented at his craft, wickedly funny, a master media-manipulator, able to command and inspire others, and shrewd... very shrewd. One of the few to know what he doesn't know – an unusual saving grace that separates him from other chefs who've tried also to be good businessmen. His dirty little secret is that he's not such a bad bastard after all."

ANTHONY BOURDAIN, BRASSERIE LES HALLES, NEW YORK

126

THE
RECIPES

STARTERS

Pan-fried scallops with a
millefeuille of potato, parmesan
velouté and truffle smarties

[Recipe on page 134]

Scallops with sweetcorn purée
and quail's eggs

[Recipe on page 136]

Mosaic of fruits de mer with
saffron potatoes, tomato consommé
and oscietra caviar

[Recipe on page 138]

Ravioli of lobster, langoustine and
salmon with a lemongrass and
chervil velouté

[Recipe on page 140]

Salad of lobster with octopus
carpaccio, roasted watermelon,
baby squid and a shellfish sauce

[Recipe on page 142]

Seared loin of tuna with poached
veal fillet, spring truffles and
caper dressing

[Recipe on page 144]

Carpaccio of tuna and swordfish
with a mixed herb salad and
brown butter dressing

[Recipe on page 146]

Fillet of red mullet with cod, spring
onion and pearl barley risotto,
and a sweet and sour pepper sauce

[Recipe on page 148]

Ballotine of foie gras with Label
Anglais chicken, marinated shimeji
mushrooms and a port vinaigrette

[Recipe on page 150]

Pressed foie gras with Sauternes
and camomile jelly

[Recipe on page 152]

Fricassée of snails with spinach,
baby artichokes, mushrooms,
pancetta and Jerusalem
artichoke purée

[Recipe on page 154]

Tartare of beef fillet with oscietra
caviar and marinated red
and yellow peppers

[Recipe on page 156]

Salad of asparagus, baby artichokes
and Perigord truffles with a creamy
truffle dressing

[Recipe on page 158]

Griddled asparagus with sel de
Guérande, served with
a tomato vinaigrette

[Recipe on page 160]

Butternut squash velouté with
sautéed ceps, parmesan crisps and
mushroom and white truffle
tortellini

[Recipe on page 162]

Chilled tomato consommé with
asparagus, peas, tomato concassé
and basil

[Recipe on page 164]

Pan-fried scallops with a millefeuille of potato, parmesan velouté and truffle smarties

THIS IS AN INTERESTING, FUN WAY TO SERVE SCALLOPS, WHICH GO WELL WITH TRUFFLE AND PARMESAN. WE PACK OUR MILLEFEUILLE IN A VACUUM-SEALED BAG TO PRESS THE LAYERS TOGETHER BEFORE POACHING, BUT I HAVE ADJUSTED THE METHOD TO SUIT A DOMESTIC KITCHEN. TO SAVE TIME, YOU COULD FORGO THE TRUFFLE SMARTIES. *[Illustrated on page 18]*

serves 6–8 as a starter

PAN-FRIED SCALLOPS:
9–12 large scallops, shelled and cleaned
20g parmesan, finely grated
½ tsp mild curry powder
sea salt and black pepper
2 tbsp olive oil

MILLEFEUILLE:
100ml clarified butter (see clarify, page 252)
650g waxy potatoes (Charlotte or Cara)
4 globe artichoke hearts, thinly sliced
about 80–100g sliced black truffle (or truffle-infused oil, to drizzle)

PARMESAN VELOUTÉ:
2 tbsp olive oil
2 banana shallots, peeled and finely chopped
few thyme sprigs
1 bay leaf
250ml Noilly Prat (or other dry vermouth)
500ml chicken stock (see page 246)
250ml double cream
30g piece parmesan rind (or grated parmesan)

TRUFFLE SMARTIES:
about 75g saffron pasta dough (see page 250)
1 egg white, lightly beaten with 1 tsp water (egg wash)
1 large truffle, thinly sliced

TO GARNISH:
handful of purple basil (or bull's blood) leaves and baby chard

FIRST, PREPARE THE MILLEFEUILLE.
Fill a roasting tin that is large enough to
hold a small 500g loaf tin with 3–4cm
boiling water.

LINE THE LOAF TIN with foil, leaving
plenty of excess overhanging the sides.
Brush the base and sides with clarified
butter. Peel the potatoes and thinly slice
using a mandolin. Arrange a layer of
potato slices in the base of the tin, brush
with clarified butter and season well with
salt and pepper. Do the same with the
sliced artichokes, then arrange another
layer of potato on top followed by some
truffle slices, if using. (Otherwise drizzle
with a little truffle oil.) Keep building the
layers, brushing lightly with butter and
seasoning as you go along. Finish with a
top layer of potato, brushed generously
with butter.

FOLD THE EXCESS FOIL over to cover
the potatoes. Press down firmly and
evenly, using a similar sized tin or the
palm of your hand. Carefully lower the
loaf tin into the roasting tin. Weigh down
the millefeuille, by placing a similar-sized
loaf tin or a small metal tray and a few
cans on top. Place over a low heat and
bring to a gentle simmer. Lower the heat
until the water is barely simmering and
cook for about $1\frac{1}{4}$–$1\frac{1}{2}$ hours until the
potatoes are tender throughout when
pierced with a metal skewer. You may
need to top up the water level with hot
water once or twice during cooking.

REMOVE THE LOAF TIN from the bain-
marie and leave the millefeuille to cool
completely in the tin. Chill for a few
hours or overnight until firm, still
weighted down.

TO MAKE THE TRUFFLE SMARTIES,
roll out the pasta dough as thinly as
possible, using a pasta machine. Place the
pasta sheet on a lightly floured board and
brush with egg wash. Arrange the truffle
slices in a single layer on one half of the
pasta, then fold over the other half to
sandwich the truffle slices. (If you haven't
enough truffle to cover half the sheet,
just use as much of the pasta as you
need.) Using a small cutter (or the tip of
a large piping nozzle), stamp out little
truffle sandwiches or 'truffle smarties'.
Place them on a plate, cover with cling
film and set aside until ready to cook.

FOR THE PARMESAN VELOUTÉ, heat
the olive oil in a heavy-based saucepan
and sauté the shallots for 6–8 minutes
until beginning to soften but not brown.
Add the thyme and bay leaf. Deglaze the
pan with the vermouth and let bubble
until reduced right down. Pour in the
stock and boil until reduced by half. Add
the cream and parmesan rind. Cook for
another 7–10 minutes until the sauce has
reduced to the consistency of a thick
pouring cream. Pass the velouté through
a fine sieve into a clean pan and season
with salt and pepper to taste.

JUST BEFORE SERVING, unmould the
millefeuille. Peel back the foil and use it
to lift the millefeuille, then invert onto a
board. Remove the foil and cut the
millefeuille into 6–8 thin slices. Heat
some of the remaining clarified butter in
a large frying pan and fry the millefeuille
slices for 3–5 minutes until golden
brown on both sides. Do this in batches
and keep the slices warm in a low oven.

REHEAT THE VELOUTÉ, add the truffle
smarties and cook for 2 minutes until the
pasta is al dente.

CUT EACH SCALLOP horizontally into
two discs. Sprinkle one side with the
parmesan mixed with the curry powder
and a good pinch of salt. Heat the olive
oil in a heavy-based frying pan until hot,
then place the scallops in the pan, coated
side down. Cook for 1–$1\frac{1}{2}$ minutes until
golden brown underneath, then turn.
Cook for 1–$1\frac{1}{2}$ minutes on the other
side; the scallops should feel slightly
springy when pressed.

PLACE THREE SCALLOPS overlapping
in a row on each warm serving plate and
lay a slice of millefeuille alongside.
Garnish the plates with purple basil and
baby chard leaves. Spoon over the
parmesan velouté as you serve, making
sure that every plate has a few truffle
smarties on top of the scallops.

Scallops with sweetcorn purée and quail's eggs THIS IS A SIMPLE STARTER

THAT CAN BE ASSEMBLED RELATIVELY QUICKLY. THE COMBINATION OF MEATY SCALLOPS, DELICATE

QUAIL'S EGGS AND FRAGRANT TRUFFLE IS SUBLIME. *[Illustrated on page 20]*

Serves 6 as a starter

SCALLOPS:
9 large scallops, shelled and cleaned
sea salt and black pepper
4 tbsp olive oil
18 quail's eggs

SWEETCORN PURÉE:
25g butter
150g frozen sweetcorn
1 tsp caster sugar
50ml chicken stock (see page 246)
50ml double cream

TRUFFLE CREAM SAUCE:
50ml double cream
100ml mayonnaise (see page 249)
1 tsp truffle-infused olive oil
pinch of very finely chopped truffle shavings

TO SERVE:
1 black truffle (optional)
lightly dressed salad of mixed leaves (frisée, oak leaf, chervil, etc.)
olive oil, to drizzle

FIRST, MAKE THE SWEETCORN PURÉE. Melt the butter in a medium pan and add the sweetcorn and sugar. Stir over a high heat for 1–2 minutes, then add the stock and cream. Bring to the boil, then lower the heat and simmer uncovered for 10 minutes or until the sweetcorn is soft. Transfer the mixture to a food processor and blend for 1–2 minutes until smooth. Push the purée through a fine sieve and discard the pulp. Return the purée to the pan and season with salt and pepper to taste. The sweetcorn purée should be the consistency of thick cream; if it is too thick, add a dash of hot water. Reheat just before serving.

FOR THE TRUFFLE CREAM SAUCE, stir together all the ingredients and season to taste with salt and pepper. Cut half the truffle for serving, if using, into wafer-thin slices and set aside, with the sauce.

CUT EACH SCALLOP horizontally into two discs and season with salt and pepper. Heat a large heavy-based frying pan until very hot, then add half the olive oil. Lay the scallop discs in the pan and cook for 1–1½ minutes on each side; they should feel slightly springy when pressed. Lift them out onto a warm plate and set aside.

NOW COOK THE QUAIL'S EGGS in two batches. Heat most of the remaining oil in the pan. Carefully crack the quail's eggs open with the tip of a knife and drop them into the hot pan. Fry for 1–1½ minutes until the whites are opaque and firm but the yolks are still quite runny. Remove to a warm plate. Add a little more oil to the pan before you fry the second batch. If you like, use a small pastry cutter to stamp out the fried eggs and neaten the edges.

TO PLATE, arrange three scallop discs on each warm serving plate and top with a wafer-thin slice of truffle and a quail's egg. Drop little spoonfuls of warm sweetcorn purée between the scallops. Place a neat handful of mixed salad in the middle, then drizzle over the truffle cream sauce and a little olive oil. Finely grate over the remaining black truffle, if using. Serve at once.

Mosaic of fruits de mer with saffron potatoes, tomato consommé and oscietra caviar YOU WILL NEED TO PREPARE THIS SEAFOOD TERRINE

A DAY IN ADVANCE AS IT NEEDS TO BE PRESSED AND REFRIGERATED OVERNIGHT TO SET. TO SIMPLIFY

THE RECIPE, YOU COULD USE ALL HALIBUT OR TURBOT RATHER THAN A COMBINATION, OR SUBSTITUTE

ANOTHER FIRM-FLESHED WHITE FISH, SUCH AS MONKFISH. *[Illustrated on page 21]*

Serves 10–12 as a starter

MOSAIC:
350g salmon fillet, skinned
250g halibut fillet, skinned
250g turbot fillet, skinned
350g centre-cut (thick-cut) tuna fillet
about 1 litre olive oil
few thyme sprigs
2 bay leaves
1 tsp rock salt
4 sheets of leaf gelatine (15g)
250–275ml shellfish stock or fish stock (see page 246)
sea salt and black pepper
2 cooked lobster tails
8 cooked langoustine tails
handful of chives, chervil, tarragon and dill leaves, roughly chopped
olive oil, to glaze

SAFFRON POTATOES:
600ml vegetable stock (or boiling water)
large pinch of saffron strands
2 large waxy potatoes
50ml classic vinaigrette (see page 249)

TO SERVE:
1–2 cooked carrots, finely sliced
few cooked baby onions, sliced and separated into rings
200ml chilled tomato consommé (see page 164)
few chives and chervil, tarragon and dill sprigs
10–12 tsp oscietra caviar (optional)

TO PREPARE THE MOSAIC, check over the fish fillets for pin bones, removing any you find with tweezers. Pour the olive oil into a deep saucepan and add the thyme, bay leaves and rock salt. Gently heat the oil until it reaches 55–60°C, monitoring the temperature with a cooking thermometer. You will need to maintain this temperature during cooking, by lowering or increasing the heat.

POACH THE FISH FILLETS in the oil until they feel slightly springy when pressed, indicating they are medium rare: the salmon and tuna should take about 15–20 minutes; the halibut and turbot may be ready in under 15 minutes. (Cook the fish in two batches if your pan is not wide enough.) Carefully lift out the fish with a slotted spoon or fish slice and leave it to cool completely, then chill for at least 30 minutes until firm.

SOAK THE GELATINE LEAVES in cold water to cover for a few minutes until softened. Heat the shellfish stock until boiling, then remove from the heat and season well with salt and pepper. Drain the gelatine leaves and lightly squeeze out the excess water, then add to the hot stock, stirring until dissolved. Set the stock aside to cool slightly.

LIGHTLY OIL a 1 litre terrine mould (or loaf tin), then line with cling film, allowing it to overhang the sides.

USING A VERY SHARP KNIFE, slice the fish fillets and lobster into long strips about the same thickness as the langoustine tails. Ladle some shellfish stock into the lined mould, to thinly coat the base. Now arrange a mixture of fish and shellfish strips neatly over the base to form the first layer, uncurling the langoustine tails as you lay them in. Season lightly and scatter some chopped herbs on top. Pour in a little more stock and add another layer of fish, shellfish, seasoning and herbs.

CONTINUE LAYERING in this way until you've used up all the fish and shellfish, then top up with a final ladleful of stock. Fold the cling film over the mosaic to enclose, then place a small tray on top (that fits snugly in the mould) and weigh down with a few cans. Chill the mosaic overnight until it has set.

FOR THE SAFFRON POTATOES, bring the vegetable stock to the boil with the saffron and 1 tsp sea salt added. Peel the potatoes and cut into 1cm thick slices. Add them to the stock and simmer for 4–5 minutes until just tender but still holding their shape. Drain well and pat dry with kitchen paper. Cut the potatoes into neat cubes, place them in a bowl and pour over the vinaigrette. Toss the potatoes carefully to coat in the dressing and set aside to infuse for 5–10 minutes, while you unmould the terrine.

TO UNMOULD THE MOSAIC, peel back the cling film covering the terrine and carefully turn out onto a board. Using a serrated knife, cut the terrine into 1.5cm thick slices. Lift a slice onto each serving plate, using a fish slice, then gently rub a little olive oil over the surface to give a shiny glaze.

TO SERVE, arrange the sliced carrots, onion rings and saffron potatoes around each plate. Carefully pour over a thin layer of chilled tomato consommé. Garnish with a few snipped chives and tiny sprigs of chervil, tarragon and dill. Finally, spoon a neat quenelle of caviar, if using, on top of the mosaic slices and serve at once.

Ravioli of lobster, langoustine and salmon with a lemongrass and chervil velouté

THIS EXQUISITE STARTER IS A LONG-STANDING FAVOURITE. I LIKE TO INCLUDE SOME LANGOUSTINE IN THE FILLING, BUT TO SIMPLIFY THE RECIPE YOU CAN USE ALL LOBSTER MEAT, WITH A LITTLE SALMON MOUSSE TO BIND. MAKE THE FILLING AND SHELLFISH STOCK A DAY IN ADVANCE. *[Illustrated on page 23]*

Serves 8 as a starter

RAVIOLI:
300g (about ⅓ quantity) saffron pasta dough (see page 250)
1 egg yolk, beaten with a pinch of salt and 2 tsp water (egg wash)

FILLING:
300g skinned salmon fillet
sea salt and black pepper
50ml double cream
300g lobster meat (from 1 lobster tail and claws)
150g langoustine meat (from 5–6 langoustines)
squeeze of lemon juice
handful of mixed herbs (basil, coriander and chervil), chopped

TO SERVE:
reduced shellfish stock (see page 246), to drizzle
lemongrass and chervil velouté (see page 248)
buttered leaf spinach
olive oil, to drizzle
8 tbsp tomato chutney (see page 250), optional
8 basil crisps (see page 248), optional

FIRST, MAKE THE RAVIOLI FILLING. Put 100g salmon into a food processor with some salt and pepper and whiz to a firm purée. With the motor running, slowly trickle in the cream. Transfer to a bowl, cover with cling film and chill for 20 minutes. Finely dice the lobster and langoustine meat and the remaining salmon fillet, mix together in a bowl and chill for 20 minutes.

FOLD ENOUGH SALMON PURÉE into the diced lobster mixture to bind it, then add the lemon juice, chopped herbs, salt and pepper. To check the seasoning, blanch a little spoonful of the filling then taste. Chill the mixture for 20 minutes or until firm, then shape into neat balls, about 80g each. Place on a plate, cover with cling film and chill again until firm. (This can be prepared a day in advance.)

TO MAKE THE RAVIOLI, roll out the pasta dough into thin sheets using a pasta machine. Transfer to a lightly floured surface and cut out 12cm rounds with a pastry cutter. Place a ball of filling in the centre of half of the pasta rounds, then brush the edges with egg wash. Place another pasta round on top of each one and press the edges together to seal, stretching the dough slightly and moulding it around the filling with your fingers to make sure there are no air gaps. Use a pair of kitchen scissors to cut around the ravioli to neaten the edges.

BLANCH THE RAVIOLI in boiling salted water for 3–4 minutes, then refresh in ice-cold water. Remove with a slotted spoon and place on a tray. Cover with cling film and chill until ready to serve.

WHEN READY TO SERVE, warm up the reduced shellfish stock. Reheat the lemongrass velouté, adding the chopped chervil as you take the pan off the heat. Add the ravioli to a large pan of boiling salted water and boil for 2–3 minutes to reheat. Remove with a slotted spoon and drain well.

DRIZZLE A SPIRAL of shellfish stock around each warm plate. Spoon a little warm spinach into the centre and place a ravioli on top. Drizzle over a little olive oil and top with a quenelle of tomato chutney and a basil crisp if you like. Pour over the lemongrass and chervil velouté to serve, or hand around separately.

Salad of lobster with octopus carpaccio, roasted watermelon, baby squid and a shellfish sauce

THIS MAY SEEM AN UNLIKELY COMBINATION, BUT THE FLAVOURS WORK WELL TOGETHER. OCTOPUS CARPACCIO IS QUITE TIME-CONSUMING TO PREPARE AND NEEDS TO BE MADE A DAY AHEAD. FOR A SIMPLER PRESENTATION, ARRANGE THE SALAD ON A BED OF MIXED LEAVES DRESSED WITH A LIGHT VINAIGRETTE. *[Illustrated on page 25]*

Serves 4 as a starter

LOBSTER SALAD:
2–3 large slices of ripe watermelon, about 1.5cm thick
2 tbsp olive oil
2 cooked lobster tails, shelled

OCTOPUS CARPACCIO:
1 octopus, cleaned
few thyme sprigs
1 bay leaf
½ head of garlic, split horizontally (unpeeled)
sea salt and black pepper

SHELLFISH SAUCE:
1 banana shallot, peeled and finely chopped
20g butter
150ml Noilly Prat (or other dry vermouth)
300ml shellfish stock (see page 246)
150ml double cream

DEEP-FRIED SQUID:
200g baby squid, cleaned
groundnut or vegetable oil, for deep-frying
2–3 tbsp plain flour, to dust
½ quantity tempura batter (see page 251)

TO SERVE:
olive oil, to drizzle
handful of mixed herb salad
1–2 baby gem lettuce hearts

FIRST, PREPARE THE OCTOPUS. Put it in a large saucepan or a stockpot with the herbs, garlic and some salt and pepper. Pour over enough water to cover. Bring to the boil, lower the heat to a simmer and cook for 1–2 hours until tender. To test, pierce the 'skirt' (the thickest part of the octopus where the head connects to the tentacles) with a sharp knife. It should provide little resistance.

RUB OFF THE SKIN of the octopus while still hot, wearing rubber gloves to protect your hands. If it starts to cool down, dip it briefly in the hot poaching water – it's much easier to remove the skin when hot. Cut off the tentacles and discard the head (or use in another dish).

LINE A 500G LOAF TIN or cake tin with lightly oiled cling film, leaving plenty of excess overhanging the sides. Working fast, trim the tentacles and arrange in the loaf tin, packing them in tightly so there is little space between them. Fold the excess cling film over to cover the octopus, then weigh down by placing a similar-sized loaf tin or a small metal tray and a few cans on top. (The gelatinous texture of the octopus will make the tentacles stick together as long as they are pressed while still warm.) Chill the octopus overnight until firm.

TO PREPARE THE SQUID, cut the pouches into small rings, keeping the tentacles whole. Pat dry with kitchen paper and chill until ready to cook.

FOR THE SHELLFISH SAUCE, sweat the shallot in a saucepan with the butter and some seasoning for 6–8 minutes, stirring occasionally, until soft but not browned. Add the vermouth, scraping the bottom of the pan to deglaze. Boil until reduced right down, then pour in the stock. Cook until the liquid has reduced again by half. Pour in the cream and let bubble until the sauce is the consistency of pouring cream. Taste and adjust the seasoning, then strain through a fine sieve into a clean pan. Set aside until ready to serve.

WHEN READY TO SERVE, unmould the octopus from the tin and remove the cling film. Using a very sharp knife, slice across the tentacles as thinly as possible. Arrange 3 or 4 slices on each serving plate to form a neat rectangle. Rub a little olive oil over the octopus carpaccio to give it a shiny appearance. Sprinkle with a little sea salt and set aside while you prepare the rest of the salad.

TO DEEP-FRY THE SQUID, heat the oil in a deep-fryer or saucepan to 180°C. A piece of bread should sizzle immediately when dropped into the hot oil. Toss the squid in the flour to coat and shake off any excess. Working in batches, draw the squid through the tempura batter and carefully add to the hot oil. Deep-fry for a few minutes until the batter is lightly golden and crisp. Drain on kitchen paper and repeat with the remaining squid. Keep warm in a low oven.

FOR THE LOBSTER SALAD, cut the watermelon into 4cm rounds with a pastry cutter. Heat up a frying pan and add a little olive oil. Season the lobster tails and briefly sear in the hot pan over a high heat, turning frequently, until lightly golden. Remove to a plate and leave to rest. Add a little more oil to the pan and fry the watermelon rounds for 1–2 minutes on each side until the sides are lightly caramelised.

TO ASSEMBLE, gently warm through the shellfish sauce. Slice the lobster tails into 1.5cm rounds. Arrange the lobster and watermelon slices overlapping on each plate, diagonally across the octopus carpaccio. Top the lobster slices with the deep-fried squid tentacles and arrange the crispy squid rings around the plate. Garnish with the salad leaves and baby gem hearts, then drizzle over a little olive oil. Serve the shellfish sauce on the side.

Seared loin of tuna with poached veal fillet, spring truffles and caper dressing

I LOVE THE SIMPLICITY OF THIS STARTER – LEAN VEAL AND TUNA WITH SLICES OF FRAGRANT WHITE TRUFFLE AND A PIQUANT CAPER DRESSING. POACH THE VEAL, SEAR THE TUNA AND PREPARE THE SAUCE WELL AHEAD AND IT WILL TAKE YOU ONLY MINUTES TO ASSEMBLE THE DISH TO SERVE. *[Illustrated on page 28]*

Serves 6–8 as a starter

VEAL:
600g veal fillet, preferably from the thick end
about 500ml olive oil
few thyme sprigs
2 garlic cloves, peeled
sea salt and black pepper

TUNA:
600g very fresh centre-cut tuna, ideally sashimi-grade
drizzle of olive oil

CAPER DRESSING:
2 tbsp olive oil, plus extra to drizzle
1½ tbsp capers, rinsed and drained
1 small garlic clove, peeled and finely chopped
1–2 tbsp lemon juice
250ml mayonnaise (see page 249)
2 spring onions, finely chopped

TO SERVE:
1–2 white truffles, thinly sliced
2–3 tbsp capers, rinsed and drained
mixed herb and cress salad, lightly dressed with classic vinaigrette (see page 249)

TO PREPARE THE VEAL, cut off any fat or sinew surrounding the fillet, then trim it to a neat round log, about 4–5cm thick. Wrap tightly with cling film and chill for a few hours to set the shape.

TO PREPARE THE TUNA, trim to a neat log, similar in thickness to the veal fillet. Save 100g of the tuna trimmings for the dressing (use the rest for another dish). Wrap the tuna log tightly in cling film and chill for 2–3 hours until firm.

POUR THE OLIVE OIL into a saucepan that is just large enough to hold the veal. Add the thyme and garlic and heat gently until just below simmering. Unwrap the veal and season all over with salt and pepper. Add to the pan, making sure that it is entirely submerged in the oil. Top up with a little more oil if necessary. Cook slowly for 15–20 minutes. For medium rare, the veal should feel slightly springy when pressed.

LIFT OUT THE VEAL onto a board, using a pair of tongs. Leave to cool completely. Wipe off any excess oil with a piece of kitchen paper, then wrap the veal tightly in cling film and chill until ready to serve.

HEAT A FRYING PAN until you can feel the heat rising above the pan. Unwrap the tuna and season with salt and pepper. Drizzle a little olive oil into the pan, then add the tuna. Roll it around the pan until it is evenly seared; this should only take 15–20 seconds on each side. Cool, rewrap in cling film and freeze for 1½–2 hours until firm.

FOR THE CAPER DRESSING, season the reserved tuna trimmings and quickly sear in a hot pan with a drizzle of olive oil. While still hot, place in a food processor with the capers, garlic, 2 tbsp olive oil and 1 tbsp lemon juice. Blend to a smooth paste, stopping to scrape down the sides of the food processor once or twice. Add the mayonnaise and whiz again to combine. The dressing should be the consistency of pouring cream; if it is too thick, add a little hot water and blend again. Transfer to a bowl and stir in the spring onions. Taste and adjust the seasoning with salt, pepper and a little more lemon juice if required. Chill if making in advance.

REMOVE THE TUNA from the freezer 10–15 minutes before you are ready to serve. Slice the tuna and veal as thinly as possible, using a very sharp knife. Leave to stand for a few minutes, so that the tuna is not frozen around the edges. Bring the dressing to room temperature.

TO SERVE, arrange the veal and tuna slices, overlapping them with the truffle slices in a circular fashion on a platter or individual plates. Arrange the capers to form a border around the plate(s), then place a neat handful of mixed herb salad in the centre. Pour over the dressing just as you are about to serve.

Carpaccio of tuna and swordfish with a mixed herb salad and brown butter dressing

THIS EYE-CATCHING DISH IS MUCH EASIER THAN IT MIGHT APPEAR TO BE. PREPARE THE FISH AND MARINATE THE MOOLI WELL IN ADVANCE, LEAVING THE DRESSING UNTIL AN HOUR OR SO BEFORE SERVING. OBVIOUSLY YOU NEED TO USE VERY FRESH FISH IN PRIME CONDITION. *[Illustrated on page 29]*

Serves 4–6 as a starter

CARPACCIO:
600g centre-cut loin of blue-fin tuna, ideally sashimi-grade
600g centre-cut swordfish fillets

MARINATED MOOLI:
½ mooli (white radish), thicker end only
3 tbsp sesame oil
1 tbsp olive oil
1 shallot, peeled and finely chopped
3 tbsp light soy sauce
3 tbsp balsamic vinegar

BROWN BUTTER DRESSING:
125g unsalted butter
juice of 1 small lemon
pinch of fine sea salt
60ml double cream
drizzle of olive oil

TO SERVE:
olive oil, to drizzle
sea salt, to sprinkle
baby chard leaves, to garnish
oscietra caviar (optional)

FOR THE CARPACCIO, put the tuna and swordfish in the freezer for 1–2 hours before preparing. This will make them easier to cut neatly.

WHEN JUST FIRM, trim the tuna and cut out two even-sized square logs, each about 2.5cm across. Remove the skin from the swordfish and cut out two square logs, similar to the width and length of the tuna logs. For optimum presentation, avoid including any brown or blood-tinged meat from the swordfish. (Use these and any trimmings from the tuna for another dish.)

PLACE THE TUNA AND SWORDFISH logs on a large piece of cling film, alternately to form a neat row. Trim both ends slightly to even up the logs, then wrap tightly in the cling film. Slide the fish onto a baking sheet and freeze for another 3 hours until they are very firm.

FOR THE MARINATED MOOLI, heat the sesame and olive oils, shallot, soy sauce and balsamic vinegar in a small saucepan until bubbling. Take the pan off the heat and leave to cool to room temperature. Peel the mooli and thinly slice it lengthways, using a mandolin. Pick out 12–14 neat slices and arrange them on one or two baking sheets in a single layer. Spread the shallot dressing over the sliced mooli, wrap the trays with cling film and set aside to marinate at room temperature for about 1½–2 hours.

FOR THE BROWN BUTTER DRESSING, gently melt the butter in a saucepan, then increase the heat and cook until golden brown. (Don't leave unattended as it will quickly burn.) As soon as it colours, take off the heat and leave to stand for a few minutes. Pour off the clear liquid into a heatproof bowl, leaving the sediment behind. Cool to room temperature.

POUR THE LEMON JUICE into a food processor and add a generous pinch of salt. Pulse for a few seconds, then pour in the brown butter, cream, olive oil and 3 tbsp boiling water. Whiz to emulsify for 10–15 seconds until you have a thick, creamy sauce. If it is too thick, add a little more boiling water and pulse again, stopping halfway to scrape down the sides of the processor. Transfer to a clean squeezy bottle and stand in a pan of lukewarm water until ready to use.

WHEN READY TO SERVE, unwrap the fish and slice across the logs into thin strips, using a long sharp knife. (At the restaurant, we use a meat slicer for this.)

SCRAPE OFF THE SHALLOTS from the marinated mooli, then cut the mooli into 1cm thick strips and trim to neaten.

TO PLATE, carefully lift the fish strips with a knife and arrange on individual square plates to form a checkerboard pattern. Rub the fish with a little olive oil and sprinkle with some sea salt.

FORM A NEAT BORDER of mooli strips around the edge of the checkerboard, overlapping them as necessary. Pipe the brown butter dressing neatly around the inner edge of the mooli and garnish with baby chard leaves. Place a few tiny spoonfuls of caviar on the chequerboard to finish if you like.

Fillet of red mullet with cod, spring onion and pearl barley risotto, and a sweet and sour pepper sauce

I LOVE THIS PRESENTATION, THOUGH IT RELIES ON USING ONLY THE TAIL HALF OF THE MULLET. IN THE RESTAURANT, WE USE THE REST OF THE FISH IN ANOTHER DISH. YOU CAN EITHER DO THE SAME OR USE 3 FILLETED RED MULLET INSTEAD. OMIT THE STUFFED LETTUCE BALLS FOR A SIMPLER DISH. *[Illustrated on page 31]*

Serves 6 as a starter

6 small red mullet, tail half only (see left)
pinch of saffron strands
olive oil, to drizzle
sea salt and black pepper

SWEET AND SOUR PEPPER SAUCE:
1 tbsp olive oil
2 shallots, peeled and chopped
½ head of garlic, split horizontally (unpeeled)
½ tsp coriander seeds
2 red peppers, cored, deseeded and chopped
½ yellow pepper, cored, deseeded and chopped
few tarragon sprigs, roughly chopped
60ml white wine vinegar
250ml Noilly Prat (or other dry vermouth)
250ml vegetable stock (see page 247)
20g butter, diced

RISOTTO:
1 litre fish stock (see page 246)
few thyme sprigs, 1 bay leaf
100g cod fillet, with skin
200g pearl barley
20g butter, diced
2 tbsp mascarpone
3 tbsp freshly grated parmesan
2 spring onions, finely sliced

STUFFED LETTUCE BALLS:
24 outer leaves from 4 baby gem lettuce, cores trimmed
1 boneless chicken breast, skinned (about 120g), chopped
1 tbsp lemon juice
2 tbsp double cream
50g foie gras

TO SERVE:
sautéed red and yellow peppers
1 tbsp tapenade (see page 249), mixed with 4 tbsp olive oil

TO PREPARE THE RED MULLET, remove the lower fin. Now, without cutting through the top fin, use a sharp fish knife to cut along and around the backbone, then snap the end connecting to the tail to remove the bone. You want to keep the top flesh and tail intact so that the fish opens out like a butterfly. Trim off the top fin with scissors and pull out any pin bones with tweezers. Trim the fish slightly to neaten the edges.

MIX THE SAFFRON with a generous drizzle of olive oil in a large bowl. Toss the fish in the oil to coat, then open out the fillets and lay them, flesh side down, on a baking tray. Cover with cling film and chill until ready to cook.

TO MAKE THE SAUCE, heat the olive oil in a pan and sweat the shallots with the garlic and coriander seeds for 5 minutes until beginning to soften but not brown. Add the chopped peppers and tarragon and stir over a high heat for 3–4 minutes. Add the wine vinegar, scraping the bottom of the pan to deglaze. Let bubble until reduced right down and the pan is quite dry. Pour in the vermouth and boil to reduce by two-thirds. Pour in the stock and boil until reduced by half. Discard the garlic, then tip the contents of the pan into a food processor. Pulse for a few seconds to a rough purée, then strain the sauce through a muslin-lined sieve into a clean pan. Adjust the seasoning, adding 1 tsp caster sugar to balance the acidity if required. Set aside until ready to serve.

FOR THE RISOTTO, heat 300ml of the fish stock with the herbs in a wide pan until just simmering. Season the cod and poach in the stock for 3–4 minutes until the flesh is opaque and just cooked. Lift out and leave to cool slightly, then flake, discarding the skin and pin bones. Strain the stock and set aside with the cod.

PUT THE PEARL BARLEY in a pan with the rest of the fish stock and bring to the boil. Simmer uncovered, stirring from time to time, for 40–45 minutes or until tender. Take off the heat and set aside.

FOR THE STUFFED LETTUCE BALLS, blanch the lettuce leaves in boiling water for a few seconds until just wilted but still bright green. Immediately drain and refresh in a bowl of ice-cold water, then drain and pat dry with a clean tea towel. Put the chicken in a food processor with the lemon juice and some seasoning. Blend to a thick paste, scraping down the sides of the processor once or twice. With the motor running, slowly pour in the cream. Add the foie gras and whiz to combine. To check the seasoning, blanch a little spoonful, then taste. Transfer the filling to a bowl, cover with cling film and chill for 20–30 minutes until firm.

LAY TWO LETTUCE LEAVES on a piece of cling film, overlapping them slightly. Roll a tablespoonful of the chicken filling into a ball and place in the middle. Fold the leaves to enclose the filling and form a neat ball. Wrap tightly in the cling film.

REPEAT WITH THE REST of the filling and remaining lettuce leaves. Chill the stuffed lettuce balls until ready to serve.

TO FINISH THE RISOTTO, reheat the barley in a saucepan with the reserved stock until most of the stock is absorbed. Gradually stir in the butter to give the barley grains a glossy shine. Add the mascarpone, parmesan and salt and pepper to taste. Take off the heat and mix in the spring onions and flaked cod. Keep warm while you cook the red mullet and lettuce balls.

POACH THE LETTUCE BALLS in a pot of boiling salted water for 4 minutes; remove with a slotted spoon and drain on kitchen paper. Reheat the sweet and sour sauce and slowly whisk in the butter.

SEASON THE RED MULLET and fry, skin side down, in a hot non-stick frying pan for 1½–2 minutes until the skin is crisp and the fish is cooked two-thirds of the way through. (As the fish is coated in saffron oil, you don't need to add oil to the pan.) Turn and cook the flesh side for 30 seconds only.

TO SERVE, ladle some barley risotto into the middle of each warm plate and place a red mullet on top, skin side up. Arrange two stuffed lettuce balls and a few sautéed peppers alongside. Drizzle the tapenade dressing around the plates and spoon over the sweet and sour pepper sauce to serve.

Ballotine of foie gras with Label Anglais chicken, marinated shimeji mushrooms and a port vinaigrette THE CHICKEN AND MARINATED SHIMEJI MUSHROOMS CUT THE RICHNESS OF THE FOIE GRAS IN THIS STYLISH STARTER. YOU WILL NEED TO ORDER GRADE A FOIE GRAS IN ADVANCE FROM A QUALITY BUTCHER, AND START THIS DISH A DAY AHEAD. TAKE GREAT CARE TO AVOID OVERCOOKING THE BALLOTINE. *[Illustrated on page 35]*

Serves 8–10 as a starter

BALLOTINE:
250g clarified butter (see clarify, page 252)
few thyme sprigs
few rosemary sprigs
3 garlic cloves, peeled
4 boneless Label Anglais chicken breasts, skinned, about 125g each
sea salt and black pepper
2 tbsp flaked almonds, lightly toasted
75ml truffle-infused Madeira sauce (see page 248)
1 whole duck or goose foie gras, about 700g
large pinch of pink salt
1 tbsp sweet wine reduction (see page 152)
50–60g truffle shavings or trimmings, very finely chopped (optional)

MARINATED SHIMEJI MUSHROOMS:
120g baby shimeji mushrooms, bases trimmed
1½ tbsp olive oil
1 tbsp sherry vinegar
2 tbsp hazelnut oil

CAULIFLOWER BASE:
¼ cauliflower, trimmed and finely chopped
handful of flat leaf parsley and chervil leaves, finely chopped
50g shallot confit (see page 250)
4–5 tbsp classic vinaigrette (see page 249)

TO SERVE:
handful of small watercress sprigs
drizzle of port vinaigrette (see page 249)
grilled rosemary focaccia

TO MAKE THE BALLOTINE, first prepare the chicken filling. Put the clarified butter, herbs and garlic in a medium saucepan. Gently heat the butter but do not allow it to boil; there should be very little movement in the liquid. Season the chicken breasts with salt and pepper and place in the pan in a single layer, making sure that they are well coated in the butter. Slowly cook the chicken for about 45 minutes, regulating the heat from time to time to ensure that the temperature remains constantly low. The chicken breasts should feel firm when cooked.

LET THE CHICKEN COOL SLIGHTLY in the butter, then drain and cut into thin slices. While still warm, put the chicken slices into a bowl with the flaked almonds and truffle Madeira sauce. Mix well and leave to cool slightly. Spread a few layers of cling film on a work surface then spoon the chicken mixture in a row along the lower third of the cling film. Fold over the bottom and sides of the cling film to cover, then roll up the chicken mixture into a tight log, about 4–5cm in diameter. Try to avoid any large air bubbles in the log. Chill for 4 hours or overnight until firm.

TO PREPARE THE FOIE GRAS, carefully separate the lobes into two halves and remove the central vein and any large connecting membranes with a small sharp knife. Try to keep the liver as intact as possible, but take out any blood spots with the tip of the knife.

SPREAD TWO SHEETS OF CLING FILM on the work surface, overlapping the sides to make a large rectangle. Press the foie gras onto the cling film, shaping it into a rectangle wide and long enough to wrap around the chicken log. Sprinkle all over with the pink salt, pepper and sweet wine reduction.

UNWRAP THE CHICKEN LOG and place in the centre of the foie gras. Use the ends of the cling film to roll up the log, making sure the foie gras evenly covers the chicken log and there are no large air pockets in between. Use more cling film to wrap the log tightly, then chill for a few hours until firm.

HALF-FILL A LARGE PAN or roasting tray with water and heat until the water temperature registers 65°C on a cooking thermometer. Lower the ballotine into the water and cook for 8–10 minutes at this temperature. (Use a heat diffuser underneath the pan to make it easier to control the heat.) Remove the ballotine and pat dry. Roll the log on a work surface to reshape it, then chill for a few hours until firm.

IF USING, SCATTER the chopped truffle trimmings on a large baking sheet to form an even layer and roll the ballotine over them to coat. Rewrap the truffle-coated ballotine in cling film and chill until ready to serve.

SAUTÉ THE SHIMEJI MUSHROOMS in a hot pan with the olive oil and seasoning over a high heat for 2–3 minutes. Take the pan off the heat and immediately dress the mushrooms with the sherry vinegar and hazelnut oil. (They can be left to marinate overnight, if you wish to prepare the mushrooms in advance.)

TO SERVE, mix all the ingredients for the cauliflower base together and season well with salt and pepper. Spoon a thin layer into a round metal cutter placed in the centre of a serving plate, then remove the cutter. Cut a 1.5cm thick slice from the foie gras ballotine and place on top of the cauliflower base. Repeat for the other serving plates.

GARNISH THE PLATES with the marinated mushrooms and watercress leaves. Finally, add a drizzle of port vinaigrette. Serve with grilled focaccia.

Pressed foie gras with Sauternes and camomile jelly

WE SERVE THIS DECADENT STARTER WITH BRIOCHE FLAVOURED WITH FRESH TRUFFLE IN THE RESTAURANT. AS AN ALTERNATIVE, YOU COULD SERVE LIGHTLY TOASTED BRIOCHE SLICES DRIZZLED WITH TRUFFLE OIL. REMEMBER TO ORDER GRADE A FOIE GRAS FROM A QUALITY BUTCHER IN ADVANCE. *[Illustrated on page 36]*

Serves 8–9 as a starter

FOIE GRAS:
1 whole fresh duck or goose foie gras, about 700–750g
pinch of pink sea salt
sea salt and black pepper

SWEET WINE REDUCTION:
50ml white port
50ml sweet dessert wine (such as Sauternes or Montbazillac)
50ml brandy
1 thyme sprig
1 rosemary sprig

CAMOMILE JELLY:
1 heaped tsp camomile tea leaves (or 1 camomile tea bag)
60g golden caster sugar
4 sheets of leaf gelatine (15g)
500ml Sauternes

VEGETABLES À LA GREQUE:
1 baby cauliflower, cut into small florets
2 baby onions, peeled, sliced and separated into rings
50g French beans, blanched
100ml olive oil
2 tbsp white wine vinegar
½ tsp coriander seeds
½ tsp white peppercorns
1 tsp caster sugar (optional)
100g shimeji mushrooms, trimmed
4 radishes, trimmed and halved

TO SERVE:
flat leaf parsley crisps (see page 248), optional

FIRST MAKE THE WINE REDUCTION. Put all the ingredients into a small saucepan and boil until reduced by half. Set aside to cool to room temperature.

FOR THE FOIE GRAS, take it out of the fridge 1–2 hours before preparing and let it soften at room temperature. This will make it easier to handle.

TO PREPARE THE FOIE GRAS, carefully separate the lobes into two halves and remove the central vein and any large connecting membranes with a small sharp knife and kitchen tweezers. Try to keep the liver as intact as possible, but take out any blood spots with the tip of the knife. Place the foie gras in a bowl, sprinkle with sea salt and pour over the sweet wine reduction. Cover the bowl with cling film and chill for a few hours or overnight.

REMOVE THE FOIE GRAS from the fridge an hour before cooking. Line a 1kg loaf tin with baking parchment. Preheat the oven to 100°C/ Gas ¼. Sprinkle a little pink salt over the base of the tin, then pack in the foie gras, seasoning as you go. If necessary, cut any thick pieces in half horizontally, to even out the thickness of the terrine. Try to make sure there are no gaps between the slices. Cut a sheet of greaseproof paper to cover the foie gras, then use a slightly smaller loaf tin (or a piece of cardboard cut to the size of the tin) to press down and flatten the liver. Remove the tin (or cardboard).

TAKE A DEEP ROASTING PAN, wide and long enough to hold the loaf tin. Lay a tea towel across the base and put the loaf tin on top. The tea towel will prevent direct contact with the tin and help to ensure that the foie gras cooks gently and evenly. Pour in enough hot water to come halfway up the sides of the loaf tin, then cover the tin with a piece of foil. Slowly bake for about 45 minutes. Remove the tin from the water bath and leave to cool completely. Place the smaller tin or piece of cardboard on top of the foie gras and weigh down with one or two cans. Chill overnight until firm.

FOR THE CAMOMILE JELLY, place the camomile tea and sugar in a measuring jug and pour on 250ml boiling water. Stir to dissolve the sugar, then let the tea infuse for 15–20 minutes.

MEANWHILE SOAK THE GELATINE in cold water to cover for a few minutes until softened. Boil the Sauternes in a saucepan until reduced by half. Strain the camomile tea into a metal bowl and add the Sauternes. Drain the gelatine leaves and squeeze out excess water, then add to the camomile and Sauternes mixture; stir until dissolved.

STAND THE BOWL over a larger bowl filled with iced water and whisk the camomile mixture from time to time as it cools. Fit a piping bag with a large plain nozzle and seal the end with a small piece of cling film.

WHEN THE JELLY HAS LIGHTLY SET (it will have a soft, loose texture), after about 1½–2 hours, spoon it into the piping bag, secure the end with a rubber band and refrigerate until ready to serve.

FOR THE VEGETABLES À LA GREQUE, blanch the cauliflower, onions and beans separately in boiling salted water for 2–3 minutes each until just tender, then refresh in cold water and drain well. Put the olive oil, wine vinegar, coriander seeds, peppercorns and sugar, if using, in a small saucepan and bring to the boil. Add the blanched vegetables and simmer for another 1–2 minutes. Tip in the mushrooms and radishes and remove the pan from the heat immediately. Season with salt and pepper to taste and leave to cool to room temperature for about 15–20 minutes.

TO SERVE, unmould the foie gras terrine by carefully pulling out the baking parchment. Trim off some of the yellow fat from the top of the terrine if you prefer. Using a warm knife, cut the terrine into 2cm thick batons and trim off the sides to neaten. Place two batons on each serving plate, leaving a 2cm gap in between them. Pipe the jelly in between the foie gras batons. Arrange the vegetables à la greque in neat rows on both sides of the foie gras. Garnish with parsley crisps, if using, and drizzle a little olive oil around the plate. Serve with slices of truffle brioche or thin toast on the side.

Fricassée of snails with spinach, baby artichokes, mushrooms, pancetta and Jerusalem artichoke purée

THIS NOVEL APPROACH TO COOKING SNAILS TAKES A LITTLE TIME. OUR ENGLISH SNAILS COME PRE-COOKED AND SHELLED, BUT WE THEN GENTLY CONFIT THEM WITH CARAMELISED SHALLOTS AND ARMAGNAC, WHICH GIVES THEM SWEETNESS AND A DISTINCT NUTTINESS – PERFECT WITH THE JERUSALEM ARTICHOKE PURÉE. *[Illustrated on page 38]*

Serves 6 as a starter

SNAILS:
2 tbsp olive oil
2 banana shallots, peeled and finely chopped
3 garlic cloves, peeled and finely chopped
250g shelled snails (pre-boiled for 3 minutes)
50g soft dark brown sugar
1 tbsp tomato purée
50ml Armagnac
30g slivered almonds
sea salt and black pepper
250–300ml melted butter

JERUSALEM ARTICHOKE PURÉE:
400g Jerusalem artichokes, washed
1 litre whole milk
40g butter, diced
100ml double cream

FRICASSÉE:
30 baby artichokes
juice of 1 lemon
800ml vegetable stock (see page 247)
1 bay leaf
few thyme sprigs
2 tbsp olive oil
300g mixed mushrooms (such as pieds de bleu, morels and ceps), cleaned and halved if large
few knobs of butter

TO SERVE:
handful of baby spinach leaves, washed
1–2 black truffles, thinly sliced (optional)
garlic purée (see page 250)
flat leaf parsley crisps (see page 248), optional

TO COOK THE SNAILS, heat the olive oil in a small saucepan and add the shallots and garlic. Stir over a medium heat for 4–5 minutes until they begin to soften. Add the snails, sugar and tomato purée and increase the heat slightly. Cook for 3–4 minutes, stirring frequently, until the shallots are slightly caramelised. Pour in the Armagnac, scraping the bottom of the pan with a wooden spoon to deglaze. Add the almonds and seasoning, then pour in enough butter to cover. Bring to a gentle simmer, then turn the heat to the lowest setting and partially cover with a lid. Gently cook the snails for 3–4 hours until tender, giving the mixture a stir occasionally. Tip into a fine sieve to drain off the excess butter before using.

FOR THE ARTICHOKE PURÉE, cut the Jerusalem artichokes into thin slices, leaving their skins on, and place in the pan with the milk and a few knobs of butter. Cook for 12–15 minutes, stirring occasionally, until they are very soft and you can break them up with a wooden spoon. Drain, reserving the milk, and transfer to a food processor. Pour in half of the milk and blend for a few minutes until smooth.

PUSH THE PURÉE through a fine sieve back into the pan. Gently reheat and stir in the remaining butter and cream. Stir in enough of the remaining milk to achieve a thick, pourable sauce. Season well with salt and pepper to taste. (This purée can be made up to 2 days in advance and kept chilled.)

FOR THE FRICASSÉE, prepare the artichokes one at a time. First, add the lemon juice to a bowl of ice-cold water. Cut away the tip of the artichoke and the tough outer leaves with a small sharp knife, until you reach the light green, tender leaves. Trim off the tough skin from the stem and base, then drop the artichoke into the bowl of acidulated water. Repeat to prepare the rest.

BRING THE STOCK TO THE BOIL in a large pan with the bay leaf and thyme sprigs added. Blanch the baby artichokes in the stock until tender when pierced with a fine skewer, about 5–7 minutes. Lift them out using a slotted spoon and leave to cool.

WHEN READY TO SERVE, cut the baby artichokes in half vertically. Heat a large sauté pan, then add the olive oil, followed by the artichokes. Season with salt and pepper and pan-fry until the artichokes are golden brown at the edges. Remove from the pan and keep warm.

ADD THE MUSHROOMS and a few knobs of butter to the same pan and toss over a high heat. Tip in the snails and toss well to mix. Sauté for a few minutes until the snails are warmed through and any liquid released by the mushrooms have been cooked off. Remove the pan from the heat and keep warm. Reheat the artichoke purée.

TO ASSEMBLE, arrange the baby spinach in a circle around each serving plate, alternating each leaf with a slice of black truffle if using. Dot the garlic purée around the edge of the plates. Place a deep metal cutter in the centre of each plate and squeeze over a little more garlic purée. Arrange the artichoke halves around the inside of the cutters with the cut sides facing outwards and stem ends uppermost. Fill the middle with the snail and mushroom fricassée. Carefully lift up the metal cutters and add a parsley crisp garnish if you like. Pour the Jerusalem artichoke purée around the spinach border and serve at once.

Tartare of beef fillet with oscietra caviar and marinated red and yellow peppers

THE FIRST REQUIREMENT FOR A GOOD STEAK TARTARE IS THE FINEST FILLET STEAK. CHILL IT WELL BEFORE DICING BY HAND, USING A RAZOR-SHARP KNIFE, AND AVOID OVERWORKING, SO IT RETAINS A CLEAN TEXTURE AND TASTE. THIS PRESENTATION IS STUNNING, BUT YOU CAN OMIT THE CAVIAR AND JUST USE PEPPERS FOR A LESS EXTRAVAGANT FINISH. *[Illustrated on page 41]*

Serves 4 as a starter

TARTARE OF BEEF:

600g fillet of beef
1 tbsp capers, rinsed, drained and chopped
1 banana shallot, peeled and finely chopped
1 spring onion, finely chopped
sea salt and black pepper

MARINATED PEPPERS:

1 red pepper
1 yellow pepper
2 garlic cloves, peeled and sliced
few thyme sprigs
olive oil, to drizzle

DEEP-FRIED ONION RINGS:

2 small onions, peeled
1–2 tbsp plain flour, to dust
½ quantity tempura batter (see page 251)
groundnut or vegetable oil, for deep-frying

TO SERVE:

4 tbsp oscietra caviar, or to taste
8 blanched asparagus tips
1 roasted yellow pepper, cut into neat squares
1–2 black truffles, cut into neat squares (optional)
handful of capers, rinsed and drained
olive oil, to drizzle

FIRST PREPARE THE MARINATED PEPPERS. Heat the grill to high. Quarter the peppers and remove the core and seeds. Place, skin side up, on a baking sheet and grill for about 5 minutes until the skins have blackened and blistered. Tip into a bowl, cover with cling film and set aside for a few minutes (the steam will help to lift the skins).

UNCOVER AND PEEL off the skins, then finely chop the peppers and place in a bowl. Add the garlic, thyme, salt, pepper and a generous drizzle of olive oil. Toss well, then cover and leave to marinate in a warm place for 1–1½ hours.

FOR THE TARTARE, trim the beef fillet of any fat or sinew, then cut into thin slices. Cut each slice into strips, then gather the strips together a few at a time and cut across into very fine dice. Place in a bowl and add the capers, shallot, spring onion and some salt and pepper. Mix thoroughly until evenly combined, then taste and adjust the seasoning.

TO SHAPE THE TARTARE into patties, place a metal cutter on each serving plate and divide the beef tartare between them. Press down with the back of a spoon to level the meat, then tightly wrap each plate (with the metal ring still on top) in cling film. Chill while you fry the onion rings.

FOR THE ONION RINGS, slice the onions into rings and pat dry. Heat the groundnut oil in a deep-fryer or deep, heavy-based saucepan to 180°C (or until a piece of bread dropped into the hot oil browns in 40 seconds). Deep-fry the onions in batches. Lightly dust the onion rings with flour, tip them into a sieve and shake off any excess. Draw the onions through the tempura batter and drop into the hot oil. Fry until lightly golden and crisp, turning once, then remove with a slotted spoon to a tray lined with kitchen paper. Sprinkle lightly with sea salt. Keep hot in a low oven, while you cook the rest of the onions.

TO SERVE, REMOVE THE CLING FILM from the beef. Cover one half of the tartare with oscietra caviar and the other half with the marinated peppers, then remove the cutters. Arrange the asparagus tips on top. Garnish the edge of the plates with the yellow peppers, truffle if using, and capers. Drizzle lightly with olive oil and serve, accompanied by the hot crisp onion rings.

Salad of asparagus, baby artichokes and Perigord truffles with a creamy truffle dressing

THIS DRAMATIC PRESENTATION IS ACHIEVED BY SETTING THE ASPARAGUS SALAD IN DEEP METAL CUTTERS TO RESEMBLE CROWNS. IT LOOKS IMPRESSIVE, BUT YOU CAN SIMPLY TOSS THE ASPARAGUS AND CRESS IN THE CREAMY DRESSING AND PILE IT INTO THE CENTRE OF THE PLATES IF YOU PREFER. *[Illustrated on page 44]*

Serves 4–6 as a starter

ASPARAGUS SALAD:
750g medium asparagus (about 32–36 spears)
sea salt and black pepper
200g mixed cress (such as baby chard leaves and pea shoots)

MARINATED VEGETABLES:
1½ lemons
12 baby artichokes
75ml white wine vinegar
1 head of spring garlic, cloves separated and peeled
100g cauliflower, cut into small florets
50g French beans, trimmed
2 medium carrots, peeled
1 tbsp olive oil
16 pink radishes, trimmed and halved
1 tsp coriander seeds, crushed
60ml classic vinaigrette (see page 249)
1 tsp caster sugar (optional)

TRUFFLE DRESSING:
50ml extra virgin olive oil
50ml truffle-infused olive oil
2 tbsp white wine vinegar
1 tbsp wholegrain mustard
2 tbsp double cream

TO SERVE:
garlic purée (see page 250)
1 Perigord truffle, thinly sliced

FIRST, PREPARE THE MARINATED VEGETABLES. Add the juice of 1 lemon to a bowl of ice-cold cold water. Prepare the artichokes one at a time. Cut away the tough outer leaves with a small sharp knife, until you reach the light green, tender leaves. Trim off the tough skin from the stem and base of the artichoke. Trim the tip, then cut the head in half. Rub the cut surfaces with the lemon half, then immerse in the bowl of acidulated water while you prepare the rest.

ADD THE WINE VINEGAR to a medium saucepan of water and bring to the boil. Drop in the artichokes and simmer for 12–15 minutes, depending on size, until tender when pierced with a skewer. Drain and pat dry with kitchen paper.

BRING A LARGE PAN OF SALTED WATER to the boil, then add the garlic cloves, cauliflower and French beans. Blanch for 2 minutes until the vegetables are just tender but still retain a bite. Remove from the pan with a slotted spoon and immediately refresh in ice-cold water. Drain well, pat dry with kitchen paper and set aside. Keep the pan of water on the heat.

USING A MANDOLIN (or a swivel vegetable peeler), slice the carrots lengthways into ribbons. Blanch the carrot ribbons for 1 minute, then refresh in cold water and drain well.

HEAT THE OLIVE OIL in a large frying pan and sauté the radishes with the crushed coriander for 2–3 minutes until just softened. Stir in the blanched vegetables and artichokes and heat for a minute or so. Add the vinaigrette, with the sugar if using, and stir for a few seconds. Season with salt and pepper to taste and chill for at least 20 minutes before serving.

FOR THE TRUFFLE DRESSING, whisk all the ingredients together to combine and season with salt and pepper to taste. Transfer to a jar or squeezy bottle until ready to use.

TO PREPARE THE ASPARAGUS, break off the tough ends of the stalks and peel the lower end. Bring a pan of salted water to the boil. Add the asparagus spears and blanch for 2–3 minutes until just tender but still retaining a bite. Drain and immediately refresh in cold water. Drain and pat dry. Cut the asparagus spears in half lengthways and trim the bases so the spears are the same length.

TO ASSEMBLE THE SALAD, put a deep round metal cutter in the centre of each serving plate. Put a little garlic purée around the moulds then stand the asparagus spears upright inside the cutters, alternating the cut and uncut sides of the tip facing outwards. The thick garlic purée will act as a 'glue' to help secure the asparagus spears upright. Put a handful of mixed baby cress leaves inside each asparagus 'crown'.

TO FINISH THE PLATES, arrange the marinated vegetables around the edge, rolling the carrot ribbons into tight little rolls. Top with the truffle slices. Carefully remove the metal cutters and drizzle the creamy truffle dressing over the asparagus 'crowns' to serve.

Griddled asparagus with sel de Guérande, served with a tomato vinaigrette

SERVING HOMEGROWN ASPARAGUS VERY SIMPLY IS THE BEST WAY TO APPRECIATE ITS SUPERB FLAVOUR. A FRESH TOMATO VINAIGRETTE AND A LITTLE FLEUR DE SEL, FROM THE SALT MARSHES AROUND GUÉRANDE IN SOUTHWEST FRANCE, ARE ALL YOU NEED. *[Illustrated on page 45]*

Serves 4 as a starter

ASPARAGUS:

16 green asparagus, about 250g
16 white asparagus, about 250g
olive oil, to drizzle
few pinches of sel de Guérande
sea salt and black pepper

TOMATO VINAIGRETTE:

2 ripe plum tomatoes
120ml extra virgin olive oil
1 shallot, peeled and finely chopped
juice of ½ lemon
1 tsp balsamic vinegar
1 tsp caster sugar (optional)
handful of large basil leaves, finely shredded

TO SERVE:

12 large black olives, pitted, quartered and trimmed
tomato concassé (see page 248)
4 handfuls of mixed herb salad
olive oil, to drizzle

BRING A POT OF SALTED WATER to the boil. Peel the asparagus spears using a swivel vegetable peeler, starting from just below the tip of each spear. Trim off the ends, so that the spears are more or less the same length. Blanch the asparagus for 1 minute, then immediately refresh in a bowl of iced water. Drain and pat dry with a kitchen paper.

LAY THE ASPARAGUS SPEARS on a tray and drizzle with olive oil. Sprinkle with the sel de Guérande and some freshly ground black pepper and toss well to coat. Set aside until ready to griddle.

FOR THE TOMATO VINAIGRETTE, put the tomatoes in a heatproof bowl, pour over boiling water to cover and leave for 45 seconds to 1 minute to loosen the skins. Remove and peel away the skins, then cut into quarters, remove the seeds and finely dice the flesh.

HEAT THE OLIVE OIL in a saucepan and sweat the shallot over a low heat until softened, about 8–10 minutes. Add the lemon juice, diced tomatoes, balsamic vinegar and sugar if using. Increase the heat and cook for 5–7 minutes until the tomatoes are soft. Transfer to a food processor, add the shredded basil and whiz to a purée. Season with salt and pepper to taste and keep warm.

HEAT A GRIDDLE PAN until it is very hot and you can feel the heat rising. Add the asparagus spears and griddle for 2–3 minutes, turning occasionally, until slightly charred and just tender.

TO SERVE, arrange the griddled asparagus on individual plates, alternating the green and white spears. Sprinkle lightly with a little more sel de Guérande. Neatly arrange the trimmed olives along each side, then place the tomato concassé in a diagonal line on top of the asparagus. Spoon a little more tomato concassé across the base of the spears, then pile a handful of mixed herb salad on top. Drizzle a little olive oil around the plate and spoon over the tomato vinaigrette as you serve.

Butternut squash velouté with sautéed ceps, parmesan crisps and mushroom and white truffle tortellini CRISP GRATINÉED PARMESAN

AND SAUTÉED CEPS OFFSET THIS VELVETY SOUP PERFECTLY. IN THE RESTAURANT WE TAKE THE DISH TO NEW HEIGHTS BY GARNISHING IT WITH MUSHROOM AND WHITE TRUFFLE TORTELLINI AND SAUTÉED SCALLOPS, BUT YOU CAN LEAVE THESE OUT FOR A MORE STRAIGHTFORWARD STARTER. *[Illustrated on page 48]*

Serves 4–6 as a starter

MUSHROOM AND WHITE TRUFFLE TORTELLINI:
⅓ quantity saffron pasta dough (see page 250)
30g butter
250g chestnut mushrooms, trimmed and finely chopped
sea salt and black pepper
1 tsp truffle-infused olive oil
1 tbsp white truffle trimmings
2–3 tbsp mashed potato (enough to bind)
1 egg yolk, beaten with pinch of salt and 2 tsp water (egg wash)

BUTTERNUT SQUASH VELOUTÉ:
1 butternut squash, about 750g
3 tbsp olive oil
2 large shallots, peeled and finely chopped
25g butter
about 600ml hot vegetable stock (see page 247)
75ml double cream

PARMESAN CRISP:
4–6 heaped tbsp grated parmesan
black truffle trimmings and/or shavings

SAUTÉED CEPS AND SCALLOPS:
1 tbsp olive oil
few knobs of butter
4 large ceps, thickly sliced
1 tbsp chopped flat leaf parsley or chervil
2–3 large scallops, shelled and cleaned

TO SERVE:
olive oil, to drizzle

FIRST, PREPARE THE TORTELLINI. Have the pasta dough ready and rest it while you make the filling. Heat a sauté pan and add the butter and mushrooms. Season with salt and pepper and sauté over a high heat for 5–7 minutes, stirring frequently. Cook off any liquid released by the mushrooms. Transfer to a bowl and mix in the truffle-infused oil, truffle trimmings and just enough mashed potato to bind the mixture. Taste and adjust the seasoning. Cover and chill for 30 minutes until firm, then roll the filling into 30g balls and chill again.

TO SHAPE THE TORTELLINI, roll out the pasta thinly using a pasta machine. Transfer to a lightly floured surface and stamp out discs, using a 15cm round cutter. Press a ball of mushroom filling onto one side of each pasta disc. Brush the pasta around the filling with egg wash, then fold the pasta over the filling to form semi-circles. Press the edges together to seal, making sure there are no air bubbles enclosed. Now curl the semi-circle around your little finger and press the tips together to form tortellini shapes (illustrated on page 49).

BLANCH THE TORTELLINI in boiling salted water for 2 minutes, then drain and refresh in a bowl of ice-cold water. Drain again and lay out on an oiled tray. Wrap in cling film and chill until ready to serve.

FOR THE VELOUTÉ, peel, halve and deseed the butternut squash, then chop the flesh. Heat the olive oil in a large saucepan and gently sauté the shallots for about 5 minutes until softened but not coloured. Tip in the squash and add the butter and some seasoning. Stir over a medium-high heat for 8–10 minutes until the squash is soft and lightly golden at the edges. Pour in enough hot stock to cover and simmer for about 5 minutes until the squash is very soft.

TAKE THE PAN OFF THE HEAT and stir in the cream. Using a slotted spoon, scoop the vegetables into a blender. Add about a third of the hot stock and whiz until smooth. Pass the purée through a fine sieve into a clean pan. Stir in more of the hot stock until the squash velouté is the consistency of thick pouring cream. Check the seasoning and keep warm.

FOR THE PARMESAN CRISP, preheat the grill to high. Heat a small non-stick frying pan until hot. Scatter a heaped tablespoon of parmesan in the pan to form an even layer, then sprinkle with a little truffle. When the sides begin to turn golden, flash the pan under the grill for a few seconds until the top is evenly golden. Remove the pan from the grill and leave the parmesan to firm up for about 30 seconds. Using a heatproof spatula, carefully peel the parmesan crisp off the pan and transfer to a tray to cool. Repeat with the rest.

WHEN READY TO SERVE, cook the ceps. Heat the olive oil and butter in a frying pan until the butter begins to foam. Season the ceps and fry them for 2–3 minutes, tossing occasionally, until golden brown around the edges. Toss in the parsley and transfer to a warm plate. Halve each scallop horizontally, season and fry in the pan for 1–1½ minutes on each side until golden brown and slightly springy when pressed. In the meantime, immerse the tortellini in a pan of boiling salted water and blanch for 2 minutes to warm through; drain well.

TO SERVE, rest a tortellini on a sautéed scallop disc on one side of each warm soup plate, then pour the squash velouté around. Drizzle with a little olive oil and garnish with the sautéed ceps and parmesan crisp. Serve at once.

Chilled tomato consommé with asparagus, peas, tomato concassé and basil

THIS IS A LOVELY, LIGHT, REFRESHING SOUP TO MAKE WHEN RIPE, FLAVOURFUL TOMATOES ARE AVAILABLE. CLARIFYING THE STOCK TO GIVE A CRYSTAL CLEAR RESULT TAKES SOME TIME, BUT YOU CAN PREPARE THE CONSOMMÉ THE DAY BEFORE YOU INTEND TO SERVE IT.

[Illustrated on page 51]

Serves 4–6 as a starter

TOMATO CONSOMMÉ:
3 tbsp olive oil
1 onion, peeled and chopped
1 carrot, peeled and chopped
1 leek, trimmed and chopped
2 celery stalks, trimmed and chopped
1 bay leaf
few thyme sprigs
1 tsp tomato purée
800g very ripe tomatoes, roughly chopped
2 garlic cloves, sliced
1 tsp caster sugar
2 tsp sea salt
2 tsp chopped basil
2 tsp chopped tarragon
1 litre tomato juice

TO CLARIFY:
200g ripe tomatoes, roughly chopped
handful of basil and tarragon stalks, roughly chopped
$\frac{1}{4}$ tsp white peppercorns
$\frac{1}{4}$ tsp black peppercorns
6 egg whites

TO SERVE:
tomato concassé (see page 248)
blanched asparagus spears, roughly chopped
blanched garden peas
basil leaves, to garnish
olive oil, to drizzle

TO MAKE THE TOMATO CONSOMMÉ, heat the olive oil in a large, heavy-based saucepan. Add the onion, carrot, leek, celery, bay leaf and thyme and cook for 10 minutes, stirring occasionally, until the vegetables are softened but not browned. Stir in the tomato purée, then add the chopped tomatoes. Cook for a further 10 minutes, stirring occasionally.

ADD THE GARLIC, SUGAR, SALT, chopped herbs and tomato juice to the pan. Give the mixture a good stir and bring to the boil. Skim off any scum from the surface using a large spoon, then reduce the heat and leave to simmer gently for 15 minutes.

LINE A COLANDER with a large piece of muslin and stand it over a large bowl. Pour the tomato liquid through the colander, pressing the vegetables with the back of a ladle to extract as much juice as possible. Discard the vegetable pulp. Stand the bowl in a larger bowl half-filled with iced water to hasten cooling. Stir the tomato liquid frequently to encourage it to cool down quickly. Wash and sterilise the muslin (as you will need to use it again).

TO PREPARE THE CLARIFYING MIX, put the chopped tomatoes, basil and tarragon stalks, peppercorns and egg whites into a food processor and blend until the mixture is frothy.

POUR THE COLD TOMATO LIQUOR into a large pan and add the clarifying mixture. Bring slowly to the boil, all the while whisking vigorously to create a layer of 'egg white foam' over the surface. Once the liquid reaches the boil, reduce the heat and simmer gently, undisturbed, for 15 minutes; the stock will gradually become clear.

LINE THE COLANDER AGAIN with the clean muslin and carefully ladle the stock through. If it is still cloudy, repeat the clarifying process with more whisked egg whites. Taste and adjust the seasoning, then chill the consommé for a few hours or overnight until required.

TO SERVE, put some tomato concassé, asparagus and peas into each bowl or cappuccino cup, then pour in the tomato consommé. Garnish with a few basil leaves and add a drizzle of olive oil.

MAIN COURSES

Line-caught turbot roasted on the bone, with a garnish of stuffed baby peppers and spring vegetables

[Recipe on page 170]

Pan-roasted fillet of John Dory with Cromer crab, crushed new potatoes and a basil vinaigrette

[Recipe on page 172]

Char-grilled monkfish with confit duck, red and yellow peppers, and a red wine sauce

[Recipe on page 174]

Pan-roasted fillet of halibut with carrot and coriander pappardelle, baby turnips, salsify and passion fruit sauce

[Recipe on page 176]

Halibut fillets larded with smoked salmon, served with candied lemon, braised vegetables and smoked horseradish velouté

[Recipe on page 178]

Pan-fried sea bass with roasted baby artichokes, borlotti beans and a cep velouté

[Recipe on page 180]

Oven-roasted Bresse pigeon wrapped in Parma ham with foie gras, creamed mushrooms and a date sauce

[Recipe on page 182]

Roast Gressingham duck breast with honey glazed baby onions and salsify, minted peas and a Madeira sauce

[Recipe on page 184]

Roasted saddle and leg of rabbit on cauliflower, haricot blanc and baby gem lettuce, with a red wine sauce

[Recipe on page 186]

Roasted loin of venison with braised
red cabbage and parsnip chips

[Recipe on page 188]

Navarin of lamb with buttered
vegetables, celeriac purée
and thyme jus

[Recipe on page 190]

Best end of lamb with confit
shoulder, Provençale vegetables,
spinach and basil lamb jus

[Recipe on page 192]

Roasted fillet of beef with a truffle
and root vegetable infusion

[Recipe on page 194]

Slow-braised pork belly with
langoustine, crushed peas and
Madeira sauce

[Recipe on page 196]

Pork cheeks with pork fillet wrapped
in Parma ham, black pudding, baby
turnips and sautéed morels

[Recipe on page 198]

Veal osso bucco with boulangère
potatoes, Savoy cabbage, turnip
purée and its own braising jus

[Recipe on page 200]

Risotto of ceps with spring onions,
grated truffle and parmesan

[Recipe on page 202]

Line-caught turbot roasted on the bone, with a garnish of stuffed baby peppers and spring vegetables

I LOVE THE CLEAN FLAVOUR AND MEATY TEXTURE OF TURBOT. WE GET REALLY LARGE FISH, WHICH WE THEN CUT INTO CHUNKY STEAKS FOR ROASTING. FOR THIS RECIPE, YOU COULD COOK A SMALL WHOLE TURBOT: SIMPLY DRIZZLE IT WITH GARLIC OIL, SEASON WELL AND ROAST FOR 20–25 MINUTES IN A HOT OVEN. *[Illustrated on page 54]*

Serves 2 as a main course

TURBOT:
340g turbot steak
sea salt and black pepper
2 tbsp olive oil
1 head of new season's garlic, halved lengthways
few knobs of butter

CITRUS SAUCE:
1 pink grapefruit
1 orange
1 lemon
200ml Sauternes or other sweet dessert wine
200ml fish stock (see page 246)
100g cold butter, diced
1–2 tsp caster sugar (optional)

STUFFED BABY PEPPERS:
3–4 baby peppers
3 tbsp olive oil, plus extra to drizzle
1/2 red pepper, deseeded and finely chopped
1/2 yellow pepper, deseeded and finely chopped
1/4 small aubergine, trimmed and finely chopped
1 small courgette, trimmed and finely chopped

SPRING VEGETABLES:
500ml vegetable stock (see page 247) or water
1 baby cauliflower, cut into florets
250g asparagus spears, trimmed
olive oil, to drizzle
50g mangetout
1 large carrot, peeled and cut into long strips with a mandolin

FIRST, PREPARE THE BABY PEPPERS. Use a blowtorch to scorch the skins until they are blackened and blistered. (Alternately, spear with a fork and turn each one over a gas flame on the hob until scorched.) Put the peppers into a bowl, cover with cling film and set aside while you cook the ratatouille stuffing (the steam will help to lift the skins).

HEAT THE OLIVE OIL in a frying pan and gently sauté the chopped peppers for 2–3 minutes until softened. Add the aubergine, courgette and some seasoning and cook for a further 2–3 minutes until the vegetables are tender. Tip into a large bowl and leave to cool.

CAREFULLY PEEL OFF THE SKINS from the baby peppers, then put them into a small roasting tin and drizzle generously with olive oil. Place in a low oven at about 100°C/Gas ¼ for about 40–50 minutes to soften.

MAKE THE CITRUS SAUCE in the meantime. Peel and segment each fruit: cut off the top and bottom, then cut away the skin and white pith, following the natural curve. Hold the fruit over a sieve set over a bowl to catch the juice and cut out the segments, using a small sharp knife. Squeeze out the excess juice from the membrane, then discard.

PUT THE SAUTERNES IN A SAUCEPAN and boil to reduce by two-thirds. Add the stock and reduce again by two-thirds.

TIP IN THE CITRUS SEGMENTS and juice and bring back to the boil, whisking until the segments break apart. Lower the heat to a gentle simmer and whisk in the butter, a few knobs at a time. Taste and adjust the seasoning, adding salt, pepper and a little sugar if the sauce is too acidic. If you prefer a smooth sauce, strain it through a fine sieve and discard the pulp.

WHEN THE PEPPERS ARE READY, cut off the tops and scoop out the seeds with a teaspoon. Stuff with the ratatouille, replace the tops and set on a small baking tray (ready to reheat for serving).

WHEN READY TO COOK, preheat the oven to 200°C/Gas 6. Season the turbot steak all over with salt and pepper. Heat a large ovenproof frying pan or a sturdy roasting pan until hot, then add the olive oil and garlic, cut side down. When the garlic is golden, add the turbot steak and a few knobs of butter. Fry for 2 minutes on each side until golden brown, using the foaming butter to baste the fish. Transfer the pan to the oven and roast for 6–8 minutes until the fish is just slightly firm and cooked through.

WHILE THE FISH IS COOKING, prepare the spring vegetables. Bring the vegetable stock to the boil in a pan with a little seasoning added. Blanch the cauliflower and asparagus for 2–3 minutes until tender. Remove with a slotted spoon, drizzle with a little olive oil and seasoning and keep warm.

BLANCH THE MANGETOUT and carrot strips for 1½ minutes, then drain well. Again, drizzle with a little olive oil and seasoning. Wrap the asparagus spears in the carrot ribbons, to make two bundles.

REMOVE THE FISH from the oven and leave to rest for a few minutes. Put the stuffed peppers in the oven to warm up. Gently reheat the citrus sauce over a medium heat.

TO SERVE, transfer the turbot steak and roasted garlic to a warm serving platter and arrange the cauliflower, mangetout and carrot-wrapped asparagus spears alongside. Serve immediately, with the citrus sauce on the side.

Pan-roasted fillet of John Dory with Cromer crab, crushed new potatoes and a basil vinaigrette

JOHN DORY HAS A WONDERFUL, DELICATE FLAVOUR THAT MARRIES BEAUTIFULLY WITH WHITE CRABMEAT AND NEW POTATOES. DO NOT BE PUT OFF BY THE NUMBER OF DIFFERENT ELEMENTS IN THIS DISH. YOU CAN OMIT THE CAVIAR TORTELLINI, HERB CRISPS AND GARLIC PURÉE IF YOU LIKE – THE DISH WILL STILL TASTE AMAZING. *[Illustrated on page 56]*

Serves 4 as a main course

JOHN DORY:
4 John Dory fillets, skinned, about 150g each
sea salt and black pepper
2 tbsp olive oil
few knobs of butter

CAVIAR TORTELLINI:
50g saffron pasta dough (see page 250)
8 scant tsp caviar
1 egg white, beaten with 1 tsp water (egg wash)

TOMATO PETALS:
6–8 plum tomatoes

CRUSHED POTATOES AND CRAB:
300g new potatoes
60ml classic vinaigrette (see page 249)
150g white crabmeat (preferably Cromer crab)
small handful of chives, finely chopped
few chervil sprigs, chopped

TO SERVE:
olive oil, to drizzle
basil crisps (see page 248), optional
a little garlic purée (see page 250), optional
basil vinaigrette (see page 249), to drizzle

CHECK THE JOHN DORY FILLETS for any pin bones, then cut each fillet in half. Wrap in cling film and chill until ready to cook.

TO MAKE THE CAVIAR TORTELLINI, roll out the pasta as thinly as possible, using a pasta machine. It needs to be very fine: if necessary, roll it out further on a lightly floured surface using a rolling pin. Cut out 5–6cm rounds using a fluted pastry cutter and place a scant teaspoon of caviar on one half of each round. Brush around the caviar with the egg wash, then fold the pasta over the filling to form a semi-circle. Press the pasta edges together to seal. Now curl the semi-circle around your little finger and press the tips together to form tortellini shapes (illustrated on page 49). Chill until ready to serve.

FOR THE TOMATO PETALS, put the tomatoes in a heatproof bowl, pour over boiling water to cover and leave for 45 seconds to 1 minute to loosen the skins. Peel, quarter and remove the seeds, then trim to get four 'tomato petals'.

FOR THE CRUSHED POTATOES, boil the new potatoes in a pot of well salted water for 10–12 minutes or until they are tender when pierced with a skewer. Drain well. While still hot, peel off the skins with a small knife. Place in a bowl and lightly crush with a fork. Drizzle over the vinaigrette, add the crabmeat and mix with the fork to combine.

JUST BEFORE SERVING, season the John Dory fillets and heat up a heavy-based frying pan. When the pan is hot, add the olive oil, then the fish fillets, boned side down. Cook without moving for 1½–2 minutes until golden brown and cooked two-thirds through.

TURN THE FISH OVER and add the butter to the pan. Spoon the melted butter over the fish as it cooks. The fillets should only need a minute on the second side; they're ready when they feel slightly springy when pressed.

WARM UP THE CRUSHED NEW POTATOES, fold through the chopped chives and chervil, then season with salt and pepper to taste.

BLANCH THE TORTELLINI in a pot of boiling salted water for 20 seconds only (you don't want the caviar to cook through). Drain well and drizzle with a little olive oil.

TO ASSEMBLE, press a layer of crushed new potatoes into a square on a warm plate (using a suitable mould if you have one). Arrange a layer of tomato petals on top, trimming them to fit neatly, then remove the mould. Arrange the John Dory fillets on top. Sit two caviar tortellinis on one side of the plate and drizzle over a little olive oil. Garnish the plate with a few basil crisps and dot with a little garlic purée if you like. Spoon over the basil vinaigrette to serve.

Char-grilled monkfish with confit duck, red and yellow peppers, and a red wine sauce

WRAPPING MONKFISH IN DUCK CONFIT ENHANCES THE FLAVOUR AND KEEPS IT MOIST. WE ALSO CONFIT DUCK GIZZARDS TO USE AS A GARNISH, BUT I AM NOT SUGGESTING YOU DO SO. PREPARE THE CONFIT AND CHICKEN MOUSSE A DAY AHEAD, AND POACH THE MONKFISH A FEW HOURS IN ADVANCE – READY TO CHAR-GRILL BEFORE SERVING. *[Illustrated on page 57]*

Serves 4 as a main course

MONKFISH:
2 monkfish tail fillets, about 300g each
sea salt and black pepper

CONFIT DUCK:
4 duck legs, about 175g each
few thyme sprigs
1 bay leaf
300–350ml duck or goose fat, melted

CHICKEN MOUSSE:
1 boneless chicken breast, about 120g, skinned and chopped
1 tbsp lemon juice
2 tbsp double cream

PEPPERS:
1 red pepper, quartered and deseeded
1 yellow pepper, quartered and deseeded
3–4 tbsp tomato sauce (see page 249)

TO SERVE:
wilted baby leaf spinach
garlic purée (see page 250), optional
sautéed courgettes and shimeji mushrooms
olive oil, to drizzle
½ quantity red wine sauce (see page 248)

FIRST, PREPARE THE CONFIT DUCK.
Preheat the oven to 170°C/Gas 3. Season
the duck legs with salt and pepper and
place in a small roasting pan or heavy
casserole in which they fit quite snugly.
Add the thyme and bay leaf, then pour
over enough duck fat to cover the legs.
Lay a piece of crumpled greaseproof
paper on top. Place over a low heat and
slowly bring the fat to a low simmer.
Carefully transfer the pan to the oven
and cook for 1½–2 hours until the meat
is meltingly tender and easily falls off the
bone. Leave the duck to cool in the fat.

TO MAKE THE CHICKEN MOUSSE, put
the chicken in a food processor with the
lemon juice, cream and some seasoning.
Whiz to a smooth purée. To check the
seasoning, blanch a little spoonful of the
filling then taste. Transfer the mousse to
a bowl, cover with cling film and chill for
20 minutes to firm up slightly.

PAT THE MONKFISH TAILS DRY with
kitchen paper, then season well. Spread
half the chicken mousse on a large piece
of cling film to a rectangle, long and wide
enough to wrap a monkfish tail. Lay a
monkfish tail on the rectangle and wrap
the chicken mousse around it, using the
cling film to make it easier. Holding both
ends of the cling film, roll the fish on the
work surface to ensure that it is evenly
covered with the mousse. Repeat with
the other monkfish tail and remaining
chicken mousse. Chill while you prepare
the duck.

REMOVE THE DUCK LEGS from the fat
and pat dry with kitchen paper. Strip the
meat from the bones and finely shred
with two forks. Put into a bowl and
season well. Moisten with a little duck fat
and mix well. Divide the duck meat into
two portions and place one on a large
piece of cling film. Spread out to a
rectangle, large enough to envelope a
monkfish roll. Remove the cling film
from one of the monkfish rolls and lay
on the duck meat. Wrap around the roll,
again using the cling film. (The chicken
mousse will help to bind the duck meat
to the monkfish.) Grasp both ends of the
cling film and roll the monkfish to
tighten and even out the shape of the log.
Repeat with the other monkfish roll and
remaining confit duck. Secure the ends
and chill for 1–2 hours until firm.

TO POACH THE MONKFISH, lower the
rolls, still wrapped in cling film, into a
pan of gently simmering water. Poach for
8–10 minutes until just cooked through.
The fish should feel slightly springy when
cooked. Cool completely and chill if not
serving immediately.

MEANWHILE, PREPARE THE PEPPERS.
Preheat the grill to high. Lay the peppers,
skin side up, on a baking sheet and grill,
turning occasionally, until the skins have
blackened and blistered all over. Tip into
a bowl, cover with cling film and set aside
for a few minutes (the steam will help to
lift the skins). Uncover and peel off the
skins, then chop the peppers.

WHEN READY TO SERVE, preheat the
oven to 200°C/Gas 6. Put the chopped
peppers in a pan with the tomato sauce
and warm through. Heat a griddle pan
until hot. Unwrap the monkfish rolls and
griddle for about 2 minutes on each side,
until the confit duck coating is nicely
charred. Transfer the fish to a baking tray
and place in the oven for 4–5 minutes
until heated through. Remove and rest
for a few minutes.

TO SERVE, spoon the peppers in tomato
sauce into a rectangular metal mould set
on a warm serving plate. Cover with a
thin layer of spinach, then remove the
mould. Repeat for the remaining plates.
Thinly slice the monkfish and arrange on
the spinach. Dot a little garlic purée
around the plate if you like. Garnish with
the sautéed courgettes and mushrooms,
drizzle over a little olive oil and spoon
over the red wine sauce as you serve.

Pan-roasted fillet of halibut with carrot and coriander pappardelle, baby turnips, salsify and passion fruit sauce THIS

PRESENTATION REALLY SHOWCASES HALIBUT STEAKS, BUT YOU CAN SIMPLIFY THE DISH AT HOME. SERVE THE FISH ON A POOL OF PASSION FRUIT SAUCE, SURROUNDED BY THE SAUTÉED VEGETABLES, WITH A BOWL OF CORIANDER PAPPARDELLE OR GLAZED BABY CARROTS ON THE SIDE. *[Illustrated on page 60]*

Serves 4 as a main course

4 halibut fillets, skinned, about 150g each
sea salt and black pepper
2 tbsp olive oil
few knobs of butter
1 tbsp each chopped flat leaf parsley and coriander

CORIANDER PAPPARDELLE:
250g Italian '00' pasta flour, sifted
¼ tsp fine sea salt
small bunch of coriander (about 30g), leaves finely chopped
2 large eggs, plus 3 large egg yolks
1 tbsp olive oil

CARROT PAPPARDELLE:
2 very large carrots, peeled
olive oil, to drizzle

SAUTÉED TURNIPS, SALSIFY AND MUSHROOMS:
100g baby turnips, trimmed and quartered
100g salsify, trimmed
juice of ½ lemon
1 tbsp olive oil
25g butter
100g shimeji mushrooms, trimmed
2 tsp chopped flat leaf parsley
1 tsp chopped coriander leaves

PASSION FRUIT SAUCE:
2 large passion fruit, halved
100ml sweet dessert wine (such as Montbazillac)
75ml double cream
few knobs of cold butter

TO SERVE:
wilted baby gem lettuce
8 blanched asparagus spears
turnip purée (see page 250), optional
basil crisps (see page 248), optional

FOR THE CORIANDER PAPPARDELLE, put the flour, salt and chopped coriander into a food processor. Beat together the eggs, egg yolks and olive oil. Add three-quarters of this to the processor and whiz to fine crumbs, stopping to scrape down the sides a few times. If the dough seems too dry and doesn't come together when pressed with your fingers, add a little more egg and whiz again. Tip the dough onto a lightly floured board and knead for a few minutes until smooth and slightly springy. Wrap in cling film and rest for at least 30 minutes before using.

ROLL OUT THE PASTA THINLY using a pasta machine, to 2mm thick sheets. Lightly flour the pasta sheets and cut into 4cm wide strips. Set aside on a baking tray, separating the layers of pasta with waxed paper or baking parchment.

FOR THE CARROT PAPPARDELLE, peel the carrots and slice into long strips, using a mandolin. Blanch in boiling salted water for 1 minute, then refresh in iced water. Drain well and lay the strips flat on a baking tray. Cover with cling film and chill until ready to use.

TO MAKE THE PASSION FRUIT SAUCE, scrape out the passion fruit seeds and juice from the fruit into a saucepan and add the dessert wine. Boil until reduced by half, then add the cream. Simmer until the sauce has reduced and thickened to the consistency of pouring cream. Strain through a fine sieve into a clean saucepan and season well to taste. Set aside.

ADD THE TURNIPS to a pot of boiling salted water and blanch for 2 minutes, then drain and set aside. Peel the salsify, cut into 3cm lengths and immediately blanch in boiling water with the lemon juice added for 2 minutes. Drain and set aside with the turnips.

WHEN READY TO COOK, heat a frying pan, then add the olive oil and butter. Tip in the baby turnips, salsify and mushrooms and sauté over a high heat for a few minutes until the mushrooms are cooked. Add the chopped herbs and take the pan off the heat. Keep warm.

ADD THE CORIANDER PAPPARDELLE to a pot of boiling salted water. Blanch for 1 minute, then add the carrot strips and cook for another 30 seconds to 1 minute. Drain well, dress with a little olive oil and keep warm.

SEASON THE HALIBUT FILLETS with salt and pepper. Heat the olive oil in a heavy-based frying pan and fry, without moving, for $1\frac{1}{2}$–2 minutes until golden brown. Turn the fillets over and add the butter and chopped herbs. Cook for a further 1–$1\frac{1}{2}$ minutes, spooning the melted butter over the fish to baste it as it cooks. The fillets are ready when they feel slightly springy when pressed.

TO FINISH THE SAUCE, whisk in the cold butter over a low heat.

TO SERVE, put a layer of wilted lettuce on each warm serving plate. Twirl a coriander pappardelle and a carrot pappardelle around a carving fork, then slide on top of the lettuce. Sit a roasted halibut fillet on top, then finish with a pair of blanched asparagus spears. Drain off the excess oil from the sautéed vegetables and arrange around the plate, with little dollops of turnip purée if using. Garnish with some basil crisps if you like. Spoon over the passion fruit sauce and serve immediately.

Halibut fillets larded with smoked salmon, with candied lemon, braised vegetables and smoked horseradish velouté THIS

DELICATE FISH DISH HAS A LOVELY SUMMERY FEEL. SLIVERS OF SMOKED SALMON THREADED THROUGH THE HALIBUT ADD ANOTHER DIMENSION, AND WAFER-THIN CANDIED LEMON SLICES LEND A ZESTY FINISH. YOU WILL FIND IT EASIER TO HANDLE THE SMOKED SALMON IF YOU PARTIALLY FREEZE IT FIRST.

[Illustrated on page 63]

Serves 4 as a main course

HALIBUT:
4 halibut fillets, skinned, about 150g each
150g smoked salmon, in one piece, partially frozen
2 tbsp olive oil
sea salt and black pepper
few knobs of butter
splash of fish stock (see page 246) or water
few chives, finely chopped
few chervil sprigs, finely chopped
few flat leaf parsley sprigs, finely chopped

CANDIED LEMON SLICES:
1 large unwaxed lemon, scrubbed
300ml stock syrup (see page 251)

SMOKED HORSERADISH VELOUTÉ:
2 shallots, peeled and finely chopped
2 tbsp olive oil
50ml dry white wine
50ml fish stock (see page 246)
150ml double cream
2 tbsp smoked horseradish cream
2 tsp lemon juice, or to taste

BRAISED VEGETABLES:
100g baby leeks, trimmed
1 baby fennel bulb, trimmed
150g artichoke hearts, trimmed
100g radishes, trimmed
20g butter
200ml vegetable stock (see page 247)
herb sprigs (such as chervil, chives and dill), to garnish

BRAISED LETTUCE HEARTS:
2 tbsp olive oil
2 small heads of Romaine or Cos lettuce, trimmed
few knobs of butter
splash of vegetable stock or water

FIRST, PREPARE THE CANDIED LEMON SLICES. Cut off the ends of the lemon and slice as thinly as possible, using a sharp knife or a mandolin. Meanwhile, boil the stock syrup in a small saucepan for 2 minutes. Drop in the lemon slices and simmer for 3–4 minutes, then take the pan off the heat. Leave the lemons to steep in the syrup overnight. (If not using immediately, transfer to a clean bottle, cover and keep in the fridge for up to a month.)

TO PREPARE THE FISH, trim the halibut fillets to neaten and remove any pin bones. Cut the smoked salmon into eight long, thin strips, 5mm in diameter. Use a larding needle to grip one end of a salmon strip and pull it through a halibut fillet from one side to the other, about a third of the way along the fillet. Thread another strip through, two-thirds of the way along the fillet. Lard each of the remaining halibut fillets with two smoked salmon strips in the same way. (If you do not have a larding needle, use a fish knife to cut one or two slits through each fillet, then stuff the 'pockets' with frozen strips of smoked salmon.) Trim the smoked salmon strips if necessary. Wrap the fish in cling film and chill until ready to cook.

FOR THE SMOKED HORSERADISH VELOUTÉ, sweat the shallots with the olive oil and a little seasoning in a heavy-based saucepan for 4–6 minutes until soft but not brown.

DEGLAZE THE PAN with the wine and let bubble until it has almost totally evaporated. Add the fish stock, bring to the boil and reduce by half. Add the cream and smoked horseradish and let bubble until thickened to the consistency of pouring cream. Strain the sauce through a fine sieve into a clean pan. Taste for seasoning, adding salt, pepper and a little lemon juice to taste. Set aside until ready to serve.

WHEN READY TO SERVE, prepare the braised vegetables. Cut the leeks into 3cm lengths; thinly slice the fennel; quarter the artichoke hearts and radishes. Melt the butter in a pan over a medium heat. Add the leeks, fennel, artichoke hearts and some seasoning. Cook for 2 minutes, then add the radishes. Pour in the vegetable stock and bring to a simmer, then cover and braise for 4 minutes until tender.

MEANWHILE, COOK THE FISH. Heat the 2 tbsp olive oil in a large frying pan until you can feel the heat rising. Season the halibut fillets and fry, without moving, for about 2–3 minutes until golden brown. Add the butter and turn the fillets over. Splash in a little fish stock and cook for another 30 seconds to 1 minute, basting the fish with the pan juices. The fillets should feel slightly springy when pressed. Throw in the chopped herbs and spoon over the sauce to coat. Remove from the pan and leave to rest while you wilt the lettuce.

HEAT A LITTLE OLIVE OIL in a large frying pan over a high heat. Quarter the lettuce hearts and place, cut side down, in the pan with a few knobs of butter. Add a splash of stock and braise the lettuce for a couple of minutes until wilted. Season well and drain off the excess liquid before serving.

IN THE MEANTIME, gently reheat the smoked horseradish velouté.

TO SERVE, divide the braised lettuce among warm serving plates and place the halibut fillets on top. Arrange the braised vegetables around the plates and garnish with little sprigs of herbs. Place a slice of candied lemon on top of each halibut fillet. Hand the smoked horseradish velouté around separately.

Pan-fried sea bass with roasted baby artichokes, borlotti beans and a cep velouté

SEA BASS FILLETS ARE MATCHED WITH ROASTED BABY ARTICHOKES AND BORLOTTI BEANS FOR A SIMPLE FISH DISH THAT TASTES DIVINE. COOK THE BEANS AND MAKE THE BEAN PURÉE WELL IN ADVANCE. TO MAKE LIFE EASIER, SERVE WITH A SIMPLE NEST OF PAPPARDELLE, RATHER THAN TIGHT CURLS ARRANGED AROUND THE PLATE. *[Illustrated on page 64]*

Serves 4 as a main course

SEA BASS:
4 sea bass fillets, about 140g each, with skin
sea salt and black pepper
2 tbsp olive oil

BRAISED BORLOTTI BEANS:
150g borlotti beans, soaked overnight in cold water
1 small carrot, peeled
1 onion, peeled
1 celery stalk, halved
70g pancetta skin
1 bay leaf
600ml chicken stock (see page 246)

CEP VELOUTÉ:
15g dried ceps or porcini
2 tbsp olive oil
1 banana shallot, peeled and finely chopped
250ml Noilly Prat (or other dry vermouth)
500ml chicken stock (see page 246)
250ml double cream

ROASTED BABY VIOLET ARTICHOKES:
100g baby violet artichokes
1 lemon, halved
few knobs of butter
50ml dry white wine
50ml chicken stock (see page 246)

TO SERVE:
wilted baby gem lettuce
100g fresh pappardelle, blanched and curled into rolls (optional)
olive oil, to drizzle

FIRST, COOK THE BORLOTTI BEANS.
Drain the beans and place in a saucepan
with the flavouring vegetables, pancetta
skin, bay leaf, chicken stock and some
pepper. Bring to the boil and boil steadily
for 10 minutes, then lower the heat and
simmer for 1½–2 hours until the beans
are soft. Add salt towards the end.

FOR THE CEP VELOUTÉ, put the dried
ceps in a small bowl, pour on enough
boiling water to cover and leave to soak.
Meanwhile, heat the olive oil in a heavy-
based pan and sweat the shallot with a
little seasoning for 6–8 minutes until
soft, stirring occasionally. Deglaze the
pan with the vermouth and let bubble
until the pan is almost dry. Remove the
ceps from their liquor and add to the pan
with three-quarters of the soaking liquor
(leaving the sediment in the bowl). Pour
in the chicken stock, bring to the boil
and boil vigorously until reduced by half.
Add the cream and return to the boil.
Reduce again until thickened to the
consistency of thick pouring cream.
Strain the velouté through a fine sieve
into a clean saucepan. Taste and adjust
the seasoning.

PREPARE THE ARTICHOKES one at a
time. Squeeze the juice from ½ lemon
into a bowl of ice-cold cold water. Cut off
the tip, then cut away the tough outer
leaves from the artichoke with a small
sharp knife, until you reach the tender,
pale green leaves. Trim off the tough skin
from the stem and base, then drop the
artichoke into the water.

WHEN THE BEANS ARE COOKED,
remove the vegetables, bay leaf and
pancetta skin, leaving the beans and
liquor in the pan. Use a slotted spoon to
transfer half of the beans to a food
processor. Add a little of the hot liquor
and blend to a smooth purée, stopping to
scrape down the sides once or twice. Add
a little more liquor if the purée seems too
thick and season with salt and pepper to
taste. Set the purée and whole beans
aside until ready to serve.

DRAIN THE ARTICHOKES, cut in half
and rub the cut sides with lemon. Melt
the butter in a frying pan and fry the
artichoke halves, cut side down, for 2–3
minutes until golden brown and lightly
caramelised, then turn over. Deglaze the
pan with the wine and let bubble until
almost all reduced before adding the
stock. Lower the heat slightly and let the
artichokes simmer for 10–15 minutes
until tender when pierced.

WHEN READY TO SERVE, gently reheat
the borlotti beans and bean purée.

TRIM, LIGHTLY SCORE AND SEASON
the sea bass fillets. Heat a large frying pan
until hot and add the olive oil. Place the
fish in the pan, skin side down, and fry
for 2½–3 minutes until the skin is golden
brown and crisp, and the fish is cooked
two-thirds of the way through. Turn over
and cook on the flesh side for about
30 seconds to 1 minute; the thickest part
of the fillets should feel slightly springy
when pressed.

TO SERVE, spoon a bed of wilted lettuce
onto each warm plate, using a round
metal cutter to create a neat presentation.
Remove the cutter and place the sea bass
fillets, skin side up, on top of the lettuce.
Squeeze little dots of bean purée around
the plate, then arrange whole borlotti
beans, artichoke halves, and pappardelle
rolls if using, in a circle. Drizzle the plate
with a little olive oil and pour over a little
cep velouté as you serve.

Oven-roasted Bresse pigeon wrapped in Parma ham with foie gras, creamed mushrooms and a date sauce AN ELEGANT MAIN DISH,

FEATURING FRESH CEPS, CONFIT PIGEON LEGS AND JUICY PIGEON BREASTS. COOK THE CONFIT, MAKE

THE SAUCES AND PREPARE THE PIGEON BREAST PARCELS READY FOR COOKING A DAY IN ADVANCE AND

YOU WILL FIND THIS AN EASY DISH TO ASSEMBLE AND SERVE AT THE LAST MINUTE. *[Illustrated on page 69]*

Serves 4 as a main course

PIGEON:
4 Bresse pigeons
250g foie gras, deveined (see page 151)
few thyme sprigs
1 bay leaf
¹/₂ tsp rock salt
sea salt and black pepper
300ml goose or duck fat, melted
4 slices of Parma ham
2 tbsp olive oil
few knobs of butter
1 quantity red wine sauce (see page 248)

DATE SAUCE:
125g pitted dates, chopped
25g chilled butter, diced

CREAMED MUSHROOMS:
200g fresh ceps, cleaned and chopped
20g butter
60ml double cream

TO PREPARE THE PIGEON, remove the legs and set aside for the confit. Take the breasts off the bone, wrap in cling film and chill until ready to use. Cut the foie gras into four even pieces and wrap in cling film. To get nicely squared sides if required, press each piece against the side of a square cake tin. Freeze for 1–2 hours until the foie gras pieces are solid.

TO CONFIT THE PIGEON LEGS, put them into a small saucepan with the thyme, bay leaf, rock salt and ½ tsp black pepper. Cover with the melted goose fat, then put a small piece of wet greaseproof paper on top. Heat the fat to a slow simmer and let the pigeon cook very gently for about an hour until the meat is tender, then take off the heat.

TAKE THE FOIE GRAS from the freezer, unwrap and season lightly with salt and pepper. Heat a frying pan until very hot, then sear the foie gras pieces for a few seconds on each side until lightly coloured; you don't want them to cook through. Take out of the pan and leave to cool, then wrap in cling film and freeze again until firm.

FOR THE DATE SAUCE, put the dates in a small saucepan and add just enough water to cover. Bring to the boil and cook for about 10–12 minutes until the dates are soft and pulpy. While still hot, transfer to a small food processor and blend to a fine purée.

RETURN THE DATE PURÉE to the pan and place over a low heat. Add a little of the red wine sauce (for serving) to loosen the purée, then whisk in the butter a few knobs at a time. Season with salt and pepper to taste. Cool slightly, then pour the sauce into a squeezy bottle.

WHEN FIRM, remove the foie gras from the freezer. Lay the Parma ham slices out on a board. Unwrap the foie gras and season the pigeon breasts. Sandwich each piece of foie gras between two pigeon breasts, using the smaller fillets on the side to cover any gaps between the breasts. Place each parcel at the end of a Parma ham slice and roll up. Wrap in cling film and chill until ready to cook.

WHEN READY TO COOK, preheat the oven to 200°C/Gas 6. Heat an ovenproof sauté pan and add the olive oil. Unwrap the pigeon breast parcels and place in the pan. Sear for 1½ minutes on each side until the Parma ham is browned all over, then transfer the pan to the oven. Roast for 5–7 minutes until the pigeon breasts are medium rare; they should feel slightly springy when pressed. Set aside in a warm place to rest for a few minutes.

TO COOK THE MUSHROOMS, melt the butter in a sauté pan until it begins to foam. Add the mushrooms with some seasoning and sauté for 3–4 minutes until golden brown. Stir in the cream and take the pan off the heat. In another pan, warm up the red wine sauce.

HEAT A FRYING PAN UNTIL HOT. Remove the pigeon legs from the fat and add to the pan with a little seasoning, a few knobs of butter and a splash of red wine sauce. Cook the pigeon, basting with the melted butter and sauce, for 2–3 minutes until nicely glazed. Remove the pan from the heat.

TO SERVE, squeeze parallel lines of date sauce onto each warm plate. Arrange a pile of creamed mushrooms on one side, using a round metal cutter for a neat presentation. Top with the pigeon legs. Trim the ends of the pigeon breast parcels, then cut in half. Arrange these on the plates and serve immediately, with the rest of the red wine sauce handed around separately.

Roast Gressingham duck breast with honey glazed baby onions and salsify, minted peas and a Madeira sauce

SWEET NEW SEASON PEAS, GLAZED BABY ONIONS AND SALSIFY ARE THE PERFECT ACCOMPANIMENTS FOR SUCCULENT DUCK BREASTS. WHEN FRESH MORELS ARE IN SEASON, THEIR UNIQUE FLAVOUR ADDS A FURTHER DIMENSION; OTHERWISE YOU CAN SERVE SAUTÉED CEPS OR CHESTNUT MUSHROOMS IF YOU LIKE. *[Illustrated on page 70]*

Serves 4 as a main course

DUCK BREASTS:
4 Gressingham duck breasts, skin lightly scored
sea salt and black pepper

GLAZED ONIONS AND SALSIFY:
100g baby onions
2 medium salsify
juice of ½ lemon, or to taste
1 tsp olive oil
20g butter
1½ tbsp runny honey

CRUSHED PEAS:
300g shelled peas
small bunch of mint, leaves only
olive oil, to drizzle

TO SERVE:
1 quantity Madeira sauce (see page 248)
wilted spinach
sautéed morels
celeriac purée (see page 250), optional
olive oil, to drizzle

TO PREPARE THE ONIONS, immerse them in boiling water for 1 minute to loosen the skins, then drain and peel. Add the onions to a fresh pan of boiling water and simmer for 15–20 minutes until tender when pierced with a skewer. Drain well and pat dry with kitchen paper. Set aside.

PEEL AND TRIM THE SALSIFY, then cut into 2–3cm batons and immediately immerse in a pan of cold water with a generous squeeze of lemon juice added (to help prevent discolouration). Bring the water to the boil, then remove from the heat and leave the salsify to cool in the pan.

FOR THE CRUSHED PEAS, add the peas and mint to a pan of boiling water and blanch for 2–3 minutes, then drain and tip into a food processor. Add a generous drizzle of olive oil and pulse for a few seconds until lightly crushed, but not puréed. Transfer to a bowl and season with salt and pepper to taste. Set aside.

WHEN READY TO COOK, preheat the oven to 220°C/Gas 7. Heat a large ovenproof frying pan until hot. Season the duck breasts and place skin side down in the pan. Cook for 3–4 minutes until golden brown, then turn and sear briefly on the other side. Transfer the pan to the oven. Cook for 6–8 minutes, then remove and set aside to rest in a warm place for 3–4 minutes.

TO GLAZE THE ONIONS AND SALSIFY, heat the olive oil in a sauté pan. Drain the salsify and pat dry. Add to the hot pan with the onions and fry over a high heat until they start to colour. Add the butter, honey, a squeeze of lemon juice and some seasoning. Toss for a few minutes until nicely caramelised. Taste and adjust the seasoning.

WHEN READY TO SERVE, warm up the Madeira sauce and crushed peas. Place a round metal cutter on a warm serving plate, spoon in a layer of crushed peas and level with the back of a spoon. Top with a thin layer of warm spinach, then remove the cutter. Repeat with the other plates. Slice the duck breasts and arrange overlapping on the spinach. Alternate the morels, baby onions and salsify in a circle around the plates, adding little spoonfuls of celeriac purée, if using. Drizzle with a little olive oil and spoon the Madeira sauce over the duck as you serve.

Roasted saddle and leg of rabbit on cauliflower, haricot blanc and baby gem lettuce, with a red wine sauce WE ACCOMPANY THIS RABBIT

DISH WITH WHOLEGRAIN MUSTARD – SERVED ON EDIBLE SPOONS MADE FROM GRISSINI DOUGH

SPECKLED WITH POPPY SEEDS, BUT A POT OF GRAINY MUSTARD ON THE SIDE WILL DO! PREPARE THE

STUFFED SADDLE OF RABBIT, READY FOR ROASTING, A DAY AHEAD. *[Illustrated on page 71]*

Serves 2–3 as a main course

RABBIT:
1 rabbit, about 1.3kg
1 bay leaf
few thyme sprigs
½ tsp black peppercorns
1 tsp coarse sea salt
about 500g goose or duck fat, melted
small handful of chives, finely chopped
sea salt and black pepper
2–3 tbsp olive oil
50g trompette de la mort (or other wild mushrooms), cleaned
85g caul fat or crepinette

SAUTÉED CAULIFLOWER, HARICOT BLANC AND BABY GEM:
1 baby cauliflower, cut into small florets
few baby gem lettuce leaves
2–3 artichoke hearts, chopped
2 tbsp olive oil
50g cooked haricot blanc (or cannellini beans)
few knobs of butter

TO SERVE:
1 quantity red wine sauce (see page 248)
olive oil, to drizzle

TO JOINT THE RABBIT, first carve out the legs. To do so, cut through until you reach the leg joint. Snap the joint back then cut the leg off. Repeat with the other legs. With a strong knife, chop off the end of the carcass inside the pelvic bone. Chop off the lower ribs, in between the saddle and rib cage, to get two small connecting racks (with two rib bones per rack). Cut the racks in two, then use a small sharp knife to cut 2cm of meat away at the thin end of the rack to expose the bones and get a French trim. Slide the knife under the saddle and cut it away from the bone. Except for the rabbit legs, wrap and chill the jointed pieces of meat until ready to assemble and cook.

FOR THE CONFIT RABBIT, preheat the oven to 170°C/Gas 3. Put the rabbit legs in a casserole with the bay leaf, thyme, peppercorns and coarse salt, then pour over the melted goose fat, making sure the legs are completely submerged. Cover with a piece of wet greaseproof paper that fits snugly, to keep the meat submerged during cooking. Put the casserole in the oven and cook for about 1½ hours until the meat is very tender.

LEAVE THE RABBIT LEGS to cool in the fat, then take out and scrape off the excess fat, herbs and peppercorns. Strip the meat from the bones and remove any fat or sinew. Shred the meat, place in a large bowl and moisten with a little of the confit fat. Stir in the chopped chives and season with salt and pepper to taste.

PUT TWO LAYERS of cling film on a surface. Spoon the confit rabbit on top and press to form a tight log, 2–3cm in diameter, using the cling film to help shape it. Wrap in the film and roll the log a few times to even out the thickness. Chill for a few hours until firm.

TO PREPARE THE STUFFED SADDLE, heat 1 tbsp olive oil in a pan over a high heat. Roughly chop the mushrooms and add to the pan. Season and toss over a high heat for 3–4 minutes to soften, then tip onto a plate and leave to cool.

MEANWHILE, separate the two fillets from the rabbit saddle. Without cutting right through, cut a slit along the length of each fillet (so it can open out like a book). Season both sides of the fillets and open them out on top of the caul fat. Spoon the sautéed mushrooms along the length of the fillets. Unwrap the confit, cut a piece to fit the length of each fillet and place on top of the mushrooms. Fold over one side of each fillet to enclose the confit and mushrooms. Wrap each fillet in a double layer of caul fat. Wrap each log tightly in cling film, grip both ends and roll on the surface to even out the shape. Chill for 1–2 hours until firm.

BRING A POT OF WATER to a gentle simmer. Leaving the cling film on, lower the stuffed rabbit fillets into the water and poach for 12–15 minutes until cooked through; they should feel firm when pressed. Leave to cool completely.

WHEN READY TO COOK, heat the oven to 200°C/Gas 6. Blanch the cauliflower in boiling salted water for a minute, then refresh in cold water and drain. Shred the lettuce leaves and put to one side with the cauliflower and artichoke hearts.

HEAT A ROASTING TRAY or a large ovenproof pan until hot and add a little olive oil. Remove the cling film, then fry the stuffed rabbit fillets for 3–4 minutes, turning, until lightly golden all over. Transfer the pan to the oven and roast for 5–6 minutes or until heated through.

MEANWHILE, fry the French-trimmed racks in a little oil for 2–3 minutes over a high heat until golden brown, then transfer to the roasting tray in the oven. Roast for 3–4 minutes or until cooked to your liking. Rest the meat in a warm place for a few minutes while you warm up the sauce and sauté the vegetables.

HEAT THE OLIVE OIL in a large sauté pan and sauté the cauliflower, haricot blanc and artichoke hearts over a high heat for a few minutes until light golden and hot. Stir in the lettuce and butter.

TO SERVE, place the sautéed vegetables and beans in two neat piles on each warm plate. Cut each stuffed rabbit fillet into thick slices and place on top of the vegetables. Cut the racks into individual chops and arrange on the plates. Add a drizzle of olive oil, spoon over the red wine sauce and serve immediately.

Roasted loin of venison with braised red cabbage and parsnip chips

THIS DISH REALLY CAPTURES THE TASTES OF AUTUMN – FULL-FLAVOURED GAME, RED CABBAGE, ROOT VEGETABLES AND FRESH CEPS. THERE ARE SEVERAL DIFFERENT ELEMENTS HERE, BUT YOU CAN PREPARE THE BRAISED CABBAGE, PARSNIP PURÉE AND BEETROOT FONDANT AHEAD, READY TO REHEAT BEFORE SERVING. OMIT THE PARSNIP CRISPS IF YOU LIKE. *[Illustrated on page 74]*

Serves 4 as a main course

VENISON:
600g loin of venison fillet
sea salt and black pepper
1¹/₂ tbsp olive oil
few knobs of butter

BRAISED RED CABBAGE:
1 small red cabbage, trimmed
100g butter
150g light brown sugar
75ml sherry or red wine vinegar

PARSNIP PURÉE:
2 parsnips
150ml milk
75ml double cream
25g butter

BEETROOT FONDANT:
2 beetroot
15g butter, plus a few knobs
1 tsp olive oil
100ml vegetable stock (see page 247) or chicken stock (see page 246)

PARSNIP CRISPS:
2 medium parsnips
groundnut oil, for deep-frying

CREAMED CEPS:
200g fresh ceps, cleaned and chopped
20g butter
60ml double cream

TO SERVE:
1 quantity red wine sauce (see page 248)
olive oil, to drizzle

FIRST, PREPARE THE RED CABBAGE. Halve, core and finely shred the cabbage. Melt the butter with the sugar and vinegar in a pan. When the sugar has dissolved, tip in the cabbage and toss to coat. Cover with a crumpled piece of greaseproof paper and cook over a low heat for about 1½ hours until the cabbage is tender. (Lift the paper and give the cabbage a stir every now and then.) If there is still a fair amount of liquid, drain the cabbage and set aside while you boil the liquid to reduce to a syrupy sauce, then pour over the cabbage and toss to coat.

NEXT, PREPARE THE PARSNIP PURÉE. Peel the parsnips and finely slice the thinner ends. Cut the thicker ends into quarters, cut out the tough cores, then thinly slice. Put into a saucepan with the milk and cook for 20–25 minutes or until very soft. Tip the cooked parsnips into a blender with about half of the liquor and whiz to a fine purée, adding a little more of the milk if necessary. Return to the pan and stir in the cream and butter. Season with salt and pepper to taste. Transfer to a squeezy bottle and keep warm in a pan of hot water.

FOR THE BEETROOT FONDANT, peel the beetroot and cut into 1.5cm thick rounds. Heat the butter and olive oil in a sauté pan. Season the beetroot rounds and fry for about 2 minutes on each side until browned. Pour in the stock and bring to the boil.

DOT THE BEETROOT with tiny knobs of butter, then put a piece of greaseproof paper on top. Lower the heat and simmer gently for 10–15 minutes until most of the stock has been absorbed and the beetroot is tender.

TO MAKE THE PARSNIP CRISPS, peel the parsnips and finely slice into long ribbons, using a mandolin or a swivel peeler. Heat the groundnut oil in a deep saucepan or deep-fryer until hot. (A piece of bread dropped in should sizzle immediately.) Fry the parsnips in batches until golden brown and crisp all over. Drain on kitchen paper and sprinkle with a little sea salt. Keep warm in a low oven.

WHEN READY TO SERVE, preheat the oven to 200°C/Gas 6. Season the venison loin with salt and pepper. Heat an oven-proof frying pan, then add the olive oil. When hot, add the venison and brown for 4–5 minutes, turning to colour evenly and adding the butter after a minute or so; spoon over the venison to baste as it melts and foams. Put the pan into the oven and roast for 6–8 minutes until the venison is medium rare; it should feel lightly springy when pressed. Remove and set aside to rest for a few minutes.

MEANWHILE, COOK THE CEPS. Melt the butter in a sauté pan until it begins to foam. Add the ceps, season and sauté for 3–4 minutes until golden brown. Stir in the cream and remove from the heat. Warm up the red wine sauce.

TO SERVE, put a neat pile of braised red cabbage in the centre of each warm plate and top with the beetroot fondant and a generous spoonful of creamed ceps. Squeeze little dots of parsnip purée around the plates. Slice the venison thickly and arrange, overlapping over the creamed ceps. Carefully pour the red wine sauce around the plates and drizzle with a little olive oil. Garnish with the parsnip crisps and serve at once.

Navarin of lamb with buttered vegetables, celeriac purée and thyme jus

THIS IS THE PERFECT DISH TO SERVE IN THE SPRING WHEN NEW SEASON LAMB AND BABY VEGETABLES ARE AROUND. THE RECIPE MAKES MORE CONFIT THAN YOU WILL NEED HERE, BUT YOU CAN FREEZE WHAT IS LEFTOVER TO USE FOR THE LAMB RECIPE OVERLEAF, OR AS A FILLING FOR RAVIOLI OR TORTELLINI. *[Illustrated on page 75]*

Serves 4 as a main course

CONFIT OF LAMB SHOULDER:
1kg boned shoulder of lamb, skinned
1 tsp rock salt
few thyme sprigs, plus 1 tbsp leaves
few rosemary sprigs
1 bay leaf
1/2 head of garlic, cloves separated (unpeeled)
1.5–2 litres duck or goose fat, melted
sea salt and black pepper
1 tbsp olive oil

LAMB LOIN:
600g loin of lamb, trimmed
1 1/2 tbsp olive oil

THYME JUS:
1 quantity lamb jus (see page 247)
leaves from a few sprigs of thyme

GLAZED BABY ONIONS:
1 tbsp olive oil
few knobs of butter
200g baby onions, peeled and roots trimmed
1 tsp caster sugar

BUTTERED VEGETABLES:
150g baby turnips, trimmed and quartered
150g baby carrots, trimmed halved lengthways
1/2 large fennel bulb, trimmed and thickly sliced
20g butter
small handful of chervil leaves, chopped

TO SERVE:
1/2 quantity celeriac or turnip purée (see page 250)
4 tsp pesto (see page 249)
150g cooked baby beetroot, quartered
olive oil, to drizzle
few chives, tarragon leaves and chervil sprigs, to garnish

TO PREPARE THE CONFIT LAMB, preheat the oven to 140°C/Gas 1. Trim off the fat and sinew from the shoulder of lamb joint, then place the meat in a flameproof casserole or a large ovenproof pan. Sprinkle with the rock salt, thyme and rosemary sprigs, bay leaf and garlic cloves. Pour in enough duck fat to cover, then lay a piece of wet greaseproof paper on top to help keep the lamb submerged under the fat. Heat slowly until the duck fat just begins to simmer. Transfer the casserole to the oven and cook slowly for 2½–3 hours or until the lamb is very tender. Leave to cool in the fat.

TAKE THE LAMB AND GARLIC out of the fat. Shred the meat using two forks, removing any sinew, and place in a bowl. Squeeze out the soft garlic from the skins and add to the bowl. Moisten the lamb with a few tablespoonfuls of the duck fat and season with salt and pepper to taste.

PLACE A COUPLE OF LAYERS of cling film on a work surface. Shape the confit lamb into a log and wrap up in the cling film. Roll the log on the surface a few times to even out the shape, then chill for a few hours or overnight.

CUT THE LOIN OF LAMB into 12 neat medallions, wrap in cling film and chill until an hour or so before cooking.

FOR THE THYME JUS, boil the lamb jus until reduced by two-thirds or until thickened to a syrupy consistency. Set aside until ready to serve.

FOR THE GLAZED ONIONS, preheat the oven to 180°C/Gas 4. Heat an ovenproof frying pan and add the olive oil and butter. Tip in the baby onions and shake the pan to coat them in the foaming butter. Season well and sauté until lightly golden. Sprinkle with the sugar and toss well. Cover the pan with a piece of greaseproof paper and place in the oven. Roast for about 20–25 minutes, turning occasionally, until the onions are caramelised and tender.

FOR THE BUTTERED VEGETABLES, blanch the baby turnips, carrots and fennel separately in boiling salted water for 2–2½ minutes until tender when pierced with a fine skewer. Drain and refresh under cold running water, then drain again and set aside.

WHEN READY TO COOK, unwrap the confit lamb log and slice into rounds, about 3cm thick. Heat a frying pan and add the 1 tbsp olive oil. Place the confit rounds in the hot pan and fry until golden brown, then carefully turn them over and fry the other side. Remove the pan from the heat and keep warm.

HEAT ANOTHER LARGE FRYING PAN and add the 1½ tbsp olive oil. Season the lamb medallions with salt and pepper and fry for 1½–2 minutes on each side. They should feel slightly springy when pressed. Remove to a warm plate and leave to rest for a few minutes.

TOSS THE BLANCHED VEGETABLES in a hot pan with the butter and chervil over a medium heat to warm through. Reheat the lamb jus and add the thyme leaves, along with any juices from the lamb medallions.

TO SERVE, put a tablespoonful of celeriac or turnip purée in the centre of each warm plate and dot a little pesto around. Place the confit lamb on top of the purée. Arrange the lamb medallions, beetroot and buttered vegetables on the plates, then pour over the lamb jus. Drizzle over a little olive oil and garnish with chervil, tarragon and chives.

Best end of lamb with confit shoulder, Provençale vegetables, baby spinach and basil lamb jus OUR LAMB COMES FROM CORNWALL AND HAS A

FANTASTIC FLAVOUR AND MELTING TEXTURE. PREPARE THE BEST END, CONFIT AND JUS WELL IN

ADVANCE. TO SIMPLIFY THE RECIPE FURTHER, YOU COULD OMIT THE PAN-ROASTED ROOT VEGETABLES

AND DOUBLE THE QUANTITY OF FONDANT POTATO. *[Illustrated on page 77]*

Serves 4 as a main course

1.5kg best end of lamb
few rosemary sprigs
2 tbsp olive oil, plus extra to drizzle
¼ quantity confit of lamb shoulder (see page 190)
4 large basil leaves, finely shredded
4 sun-blushed tomatoes in oil, drained and finely chopped
4 olives, pitted and finely chopped
2–3 tbsp garlic-infused olive oil
sea salt and black pepper

BASIL LAMB JUS:
600ml lamb jus (see page 247)
small bunch of basil, leaves finely shredded

PAN-ROASTED ROOT VEGETABLES:
juice of 1 lemon
1 salsify
1 small celeriac
1 small kohlrabi
3 tbsp olive oil
few knobs of butter

FONDANT POTATOES:
1 large (or 2 medium) potato
2 tbsp olive oil
25g salted butter, diced
100ml vegetable stock (see page 247) or chicken stock (see page 246)

PROVENÇALE VEGETABLES:
2 tbsp olive oil
½ each large red and yellow pepper, deseeded and cut into squares
½ small aubergine, trimmed and cut into squares
1 small courgette, trimmed and cut into squares

TO SERVE:
wilted spinach
celeriac purée (see page 250), optional
2–3 tbsp garlic-infused olive oil, to drizzle

TO PREPARE THE LAMB, bone out the best end of lamb, or get your butcher to do so, using the bones to make the lamb jus. Trim the meat (which we refer to as a cannon of lamb) into a neat log. Place on a tray, top with the rosemary and drizzle over a little olive oil. Wrap the tray in cling film and chill until ready to cook.

PUT THE CONFIT LAMB in a bowl and add the basil, tomatoes and olives. Mix well, moistening with 2–3 tbsp of garlic oil and seasoning with salt and pepper to taste. Lay a piece of cling film on a clean surface and spoon the confit lamb on top in a thin cylinder. Press the lamb into a thin log, about 2cm in diameter, and wrap tightly in the cling film. Chill for a few hours to set the shape.

BOIL THE LAMB JUS until reduced to a syrupy consistency. Set aside.

TO PREPARE THE ROOT VEGETABLES, add the lemon juice to a bowl of water. Peel the salsify, dice and immediately immerse in the water. Peel the celeriac and kohlrabi and cut into 1cm cubes. Heat a sauté pan over a high heat and add the olive oil. Fry the kohlrabi for 3–4 minutes, then add the celeriac and fry for a further 2 minutes. In the meantime, drain the salsify and pat dry with kitchen paper. Add to the pan with a few knobs of butter and fry for another 5–6 minutes, tossing frequently, until golden brown and tender. Season well to taste, then keep warm in a low oven.

FOR THE FONDANT POTATOES, peel the potato and cut into 1.5cm thick discs. Heat the olive oil and butter in a large sauté pan. Season the potato and fry for 2 minutes on each side or until golden brown. Pour in the stock and bring to the boil. Dot the potatoes with the butter, then partially cover with a piece of greaseproof paper. Simmer gently, without turning, for 10–12 minutes until the stock is absorbed and the potatoes are tender. Keep warm in a low oven.

WHEN READY TO COOK, preheat the oven to 200°C/Gas 6. Heat an ovenproof frying pan and add 1 tbsp olive oil. Season the cannon of lamb and fry, turning frequently, for 4–5 minutes or until browned all over. Transfer the pan to the oven and roast for 6–8 minutes until the lamb is medium rare. It should feel slightly springy when pressed.

WHILE THE LAMB IS IN THE OVEN, cook the Provençale vegetables. Heat the olive oil in a sauté pan. Season the peppers and aubergine, then add to the pan and sauté for 2 minutes. Add the courgette, season well and cook for a further 3–5 minutes until the vegetables are just tender.

MEANWHILE, heat another frying pan with 1 tbsp oil. Unwrap the confit lamb log and cut into 2cm pieces. Fry, cut side down, for 2 minutes until golden brown. Turn over and brown the other side. Remove from the pan and keep warm.

REST THE CANNON OF LAMB in a warm place for a few minutes. Reheat the lamb jus and add the basil leaves.

TO SERVE, place a round metal cutter on each warm plate. Spoon in a layer of warm spinach, then a layer of pan-roasted root vegetables. Put one or two slices of potato fondant on top. Cut the cannon of lamb into thick pieces and arrange on top of the potatoes. Arrange the Provençale vegetables and confit lamb around the plates. Add little dollops of celeriac purée, if using, and drizzle with a little garlic-infused olive oil. Serve with the basil lamb jus.

Roasted fillet of beef with a truffle and root vegetable infusion

I USE PRIME BEEF FROM NORTHUMBERLAND FOR THIS DISH. THE TIME-CONSUMING ELEMENTS ARE THE

BRAISED SHIN AND BEEF CONSOMMÉ, BUT YOU CAN MAKE THESE A DAY AHEAD. IN THE RESTAURANT,

WE PREPARE THE INFUSION IN A GLASS TEAPOT WITH AN INFUSER AND POUR IT OVER THE BEEF AS WE

SERVE IT. *[Illustrated on page 82]*

Serves 4–6 as a main course

BRAISED SHIN OF BEEF:
650g boned shin of beef, in one piece
3 tbsp olive oil
sea salt and black pepper
1 large carrot, peeled and chopped
1 large onion, peeled and chopped
2 celery stalks, trimmed and chopped
2 bay leaves, few thyme sprigs
500ml red wine
about 1.5 litres veal stock (see page 247)

TO CLARIFY THE STOCK:
200g beef trimmings, chopped
1 thyme sprig, leaves only
1 rosemary sprig, leaves only
4 egg whites
¹/₂ tsp black peppercorns

TRUFFLE AND ROOT VEGETABLE INFUSION:
2 pea pods, finely sliced
2 asparagus tips, finely sliced lengthways
2 baby morels, sliced
2 radishes, finely sliced
2 baby carrots, peeled and finely sliced
small bouquet garni (thyme sprig, rosemary sprig, bay leaf)
few truffle slices, or 1 tsp truffle trimmings

BEEF FILLET:
500g fillet of beef, trimmed
2 tbsp olive oil

VEGETABLE GARNISH:
¹/₂ kohlrabi, peeled and diced
100g baby carrots, scrubbed and cut into 5mm rounds
50g peas
50g baby morels, cleaned and trimmed
handful of cooked orrechiette (or other pasta shapes), optional
¹/₂ head of Savoy cabbage, shredded and wilted

FOR THE BRAISED SHIN of beef, heat half the olive oil in a large heavy-based pan or casserole. Season the beef and fry for 2 minutes on each side until evenly browned. Remove to a plate. Add the rest of the oil to the pan, then the vegetables and herbs. Cook, stirring occasionally, for 4–6 minutes until the vegetables are soft. Deglaze the pan with the wine and boil until reduced by half. Pour in the stock and return the beef to the pan. Top up with a little water as necessary to cover the shin. Bring to a simmer, then turn the heat right down. Cover with a piece of wet greaseproof paper and cook very gently for 2–3 hours until the beef is very tender. Leave to cool in the braising stock.

TAKE OUT THE BEEF and set aside. Strain the braising stock through a fine chinois into a clean wide pan, pressing down on the vegetables in the chinois with the back of a ladle to extract as much juice as possible. Place over a medium heat and boil the stock until reduced to about 1 litre. Leave to cool.

FINELY SHRED THE BEEF and place in a bowl. Add enough of the stock to moisten the meat and season generously to taste. While still warm, divide into 100g portions and place each one in a small resealable plastic bag. Press each bag on the work surface to flatten and use a rolling pin to even out the thickness of the beef throughout. Chill overnight, until the beef and gelatinous stock has set into a thin rectangular disc.

NEXT, CLARIFY THE STOCK. Put the beef trimmings, herbs, egg whites and peppercorns into a food processor and blitz for a minute, then tip into the pan containing the cooled beef stock. Slowly bring the stock to the boil, whisking continuously with a balloon whisk. The egg white mix will form a frothy crust on the surface of the liquid. Line a colander with a wet piece of muslin and set it over a large bowl. Ladle the stock through, letting it drip through slowly. It should now be clear; if it is not, repeat the clarification process once more using more egg whites. Set this beef consommé aside until ready to serve.

FOR THE VEGETABLE GARNISH, blanch the kohlrabi, carrots and peas in boiling salted water for 2–3 minutes until just tender. Drain and refresh under cold running water, then set aside.

BEFORE SERVING, remove the braised shin rectangles from the fridge and bring to room temperature.

TO COOK THE BEEF FILLET, preheat the oven to 200°C/Gas 6. Heat the olive oil in an ovenproof pan until hot. Season the beef fillet with salt and pepper and sear, turning, until browned all over. Transfer the pan to the oven and cook for another 4–6 minutes until the meat feels slightly springy when pressed.

MEANWHILE, FOR THE INFUSION, bring the beef consommé to the boil in a pan. Take off the heat and add the sliced vegetables, bouquet garni and truffle. Cover and leave to infuse for a few minutes, then strain. Reheat if necessary.

WHEN THE BEEF FILLET IS COOKED, remove and rest in a warm place for a few minutes. Blanch the kohlrabi, carrots and peas, and pasta if using, in boiling water for 1–2 minutes to reheat.

TO SERVE, put a neat pile of hot cabbage in the centre of each warm plate, using a square metal cutter to create a neat presentation if you like, then remove the cutter. Unwrap the beef shin and lay on the cabbage. Pour over a little of the consommé to soften the beef and warm it. Thinly slice the beef fillet and place on top of the shin. Arrange the blanched vegetables, and pasta if using, around the plates. Pour over the remaining beef consommé as you serve.

Slow-braised pork belly with langoustine, crushed peas and Madeira sauce

IN THE RESTAURANT WE ACCOMPANY THIS DISH WITH LACED PORK CRISPS, MADE BY PRESSING THIN STRIPS OF PORK FAT AND RIND BETWEEN HEAVY TRAYS AND ROASTING THEM UNTIL CRISP. BRAISE THE PORK AND PRESS THE MEAT OVERNIGHT; MAKE THE SAUCE A DAY AHEAD AS WELL – LEAVING YOU AN EASY DISH TO FINISH JUST BEFORE SERVING. *[Illustrated on page 85]*

Serves 4–6 as a main course

BRAISED PORK BELLY:
1 pork belly joint, about 1kg, boned and skinned
sea salt and black pepper
3 tbsp olive oil
1 large carrot, peeled and chopped
1 onion, peeled and chopped
1 leek, white part chopped
1 celery stalk, trimmed and chopped
few rosemary sprigs
few thyme sprigs
2 bay leaves
250ml dry white wine
750ml veal stock (see page 247)
750ml chicken stock (see page 246)
500ml Madeira

CRUSHED PEAS:
300g shelled peas
small bunch of mint, leaves only
olive oil, to drizzle

LANGOUSTINE:
8–10 langoustines, shelled and cleaned, coral reserved
2 tbsp olive oil

TO SERVE:
olive oil, to drizzle

TRIM THE PORK, reducing the thicker areas to even out the thickness. Rub all over with salt and pepper, then roll up and tie into a neat log. Heat 2 tbsp olive oil in a heavy-based pan or cast-iron casserole. Add the pork and fry, turning occasionally, for 8 minutes, until browned all over. Remove and set aside.

DRAIN OFF THE EXCESS OIL and fat from the pan, then add the carrot, onion, leek, celery and herbs. Stir over a high heat for 5–6 minutes until the vegetables take on a little colour and begin to soften. Deglaze the pan with the wine and let bubble until almost totally reduced. Return the pork to the pan. Pour in the veal and chicken stocks and bring to the boil. Reduce the heat to a low simmer and braise the pork slowly for 2½–3 hours, turning occasionally, until it is very tender. There should be little resistance when a metal skewer is pushed into the centre of the joint.

WHILE STILL HOT, take the pork out of the braising stock and remove the string. Unroll the joint and lay it flat on a large baking tray. Place another tray on top and weigh down with a few heavy cans. Let it cool completely, then transfer to the fridge and chill for 4–6 hours or overnight to set the shape.

PASS THE BRAISING STOCK through a fine sieve into a clean pan, pushing down on the vegetables to extract as much juice as possible. Bring to the boil and let bubble until reduced by two-thirds.

IN ANOTHER SAUCEPAN, boil the Madeira to reduce by half, then add to the reduced stock. This sauce should have a slightly syrupy consistency; if it seems too thin, boil to reduce and thicken further. Season with salt and pepper to taste.

FOR THE CRUSHED PEAS, add the peas and mint to a pan of boiling water and blanch for 2–3 minutes, then drain and tip into a food processor. Add a generous drizzle of olive oil and pulse for a few seconds until lightly crushed, but not puréed. Season generously with salt and pepper to taste.

WHEN READY TO SERVE, uncover the pork belly and score the skin in a criss-cross pattern, then cut into 3–4cm thick squares. Rub the langoustine tails with the coral (from the small sac in the head) to enhance the flavour and give them a bright pink coating.

HEAT A HEAVY-BASED FRYING PAN until very hot and add 1 tbsp olive oil. Pan-fry the pork squares in batches until golden brown on both sides. Warm up the crushed peas and the Madeira sauce.

HEAT ANOTHER FRYING PAN and add 2 tbsp olive oil. Season the langoustine tails with salt and pepper and fry for 2 minutes each side until just cooked through. They will turn opaque and feel slightly springy when ready.

TO SERVE, arrange an alternating row of pork belly squares and langoustine tails on each warm serving plate. Place a quenelle of crushed peas at each end. Drizzle a little olive oil and the Madeira sauce around the plates. Serve at once, handing the rest of the Madeira sauce around separately.

Pork cheeks with pork fillet wrapped in Parma ham, black pudding, baby turnips and sautéed morels

THIS IS A REAL CELEBRATION OF THE PIG. SLOW-COOKED PORK CHEEKS, ENCRUSTED IN CRISPY POTATO, ARE SERVED WITH PARMA HAM-WRAPPED PORK FILLETS AND BLACK PUDDING. MAKE THE SAUCE AND PREPARE THE WRAPPED PORK CHEEKS AND FILLETS UP TO A DAY AHEAD, LEAVING YOU AN EASY DISH TO ASSEMBLE. *[Illustrated on page 86]*

Serves 4 as a main course

PORK CHEEKS:
8 pork cheeks
sea salt and black pepper
3 garlic cloves, split (unpeeled)
1 bay leaf
few thyme sprigs
600g duck or goose fat, melted (approximately)
2 large waxy potatoes
groundnut oil, for frying

PORK FILLET:
450g pork fillet
4 slices of Parma ham
1½ tbsp olive oil

BLACK PUDDING AND SAUTÉED MORELS:
100g morels, washed and trimmed
few knobs of butter
1 tbsp olive oil
200g black pudding, cut into bite-sized pieces

TO SERVE:
150g baby turnips, trimmed and halved
1 quantity Madeira sauce (see page 248)
knob of butter
wilted spinach
turnip purée (see page 250), optional

FIRST, CONFIT THE PORK CHEEKS. Season the cheeks and put them in a small saucepan with the garlic, bay leaf and thyme. Pour over enough duck fat to cover and lay a piece of wet greaseproof paper that fits snugly on top, to keep the pork cheeks submerged. Place over a low heat and cook slowly for 1–1½ hours until soft and tender. Leave the pork cheeks to cool in the fat.

TRIM THE PORK FILLET so that it is evenly thick throughout, then season with salt and pepper. (Use the trimmings to make the Madeira sauce.) Arrange the Parma ham slices on a work surface, overlapping the sides a little to form a sheet. Place the pork fillet on one end and roll up, so that the Parma ham wraps around the fillet. If you are not cooking immediately, wrap in cling film and chill.

REMOVE THE PORK CHEEKS from the fat and pat dry with kitchen paper. Peel and thinly slice the potatoes using a mandolin. Stack a few slices on top of each other and slice into long strips, then wrap the potato strips around the pork cheeks. To do so, put a thin layer of potato strips on a small piece of cling film, then place a pork cheek on one end. Roll up the cling film to cover the pork cheek with the potatoes. Squeeze gently so that the potato holds together around the meat. Repeat with the remaining pork cheeks and potato. Chill, unless cooking immediately.

BLANCH THE BABY TURNIPS in boiling salted water for 3 minutes. Drain, refresh in cold water, then drain again and set aside.

WHEN READY TO COOK, preheat the oven to 200°C/Gas 6 for the pork fillets. Heat a large ovenproof pan and add the olive oil. Fry the Parma-wrapped fillets, turning occasionally, for 3–4 minutes until browned all over. Transfer the pan to the oven and roast for 8–10 minutes until just cooked through; the meat should feel just firm. Leave to rest in a warm place for 5 minutes before slicing.

MEANWHILE, HEAT A THIN LAYER of groundnut oil in a frying pan. Carefully remove the cling film from the potato-wrapped pork cheeks and place them in the hot pan. Sauté for 2–3 minutes on each side until the potatoes are golden brown and crisp. Tilt the pan slightly and spoon the hot oil over the potatoes as they cook. Drain on kitchen paper and sprinkle with sea salt. Keep warm.

WHILE THE PORK IS COOKING, add the morels to a hot pan with a few knobs of butter. Season and sauté on a medium-high heat for 3–4 minutes. Transfer to a warm plate and set aside. Add a little olive oil to the pan and fry the black pudding for 6–8 minutes, turning occasionally. Warm the Madeira sauce. Toss the baby turnips with a knob of butter and some seasoning in a hot pan to heat through. Have the spinach ready.

TO SERVE, PILE THE WARM SPINACH into round metal cutters on warm plates. Add the black pudding and sautéed morels, arranging the mushrooms so that their stemmed sides are facing outwards. Remove the cutters. Thickly slice the pork fillet and place with the crispy pork cheeks in the centre of the mushrooms. Arrange the turnip halves around the plates and intersperse with little dollops of turnip purée, if using. Pour over the Madeira sauce to serve.

Veal osso bucco with boulangère potatoes, Savoy cabbage, turnip purée and its own braising jus

OSSO BUCCO MUST BE COOKED VERY GENTLY TO ENSURE A MELTINGLY TENDER RESULT. IN THE RESTAURANT, WE COOK IT IN A SEALED VACUUM PACK IMMERSED IN A WATER BATH FOR 4 HOURS, BUT YOU CAN ACHIEVE AN EXCELLENT RESULT AT HOME PROVIDED YOU MAINTAIN A VERY LOW HEAT – THE SURFACE OF THE LIQUOR SHOULD BARELY MOVE. THE OSSO BUCCO TASTES EVEN BETTER IF IT IS MADE A DAY AHEAD. *[Illustrated on page 87]*

Serves 4 as a main course

OSSO BUCCO:
4 veal knuckle (osso bucco) steaks, about 350g each, with bone and marrow
sea salt and black pepper
3 tbsp olive oil
1 large onion, peeled and chopped
1 large carrot, peeled and chopped
3 garlic cloves, peeled and sliced
1 bay leaf
few thyme sprigs
1 tbsp tomato purée
200ml dry white wine
800ml veal stock (see page 247)

POMMES BOULANGÈRE:
250ml chicken stock (see page 246)
5 garlic cloves, peeled
few thyme sprigs
few rosemary sprigs
2 tbsp olive oil, plus extra to brush
2 banana shallots, peeled and finely chopped
200g (about 4 medium) potatoes
25g butter, diced

GLAZED BABY ONIONS:
1 tbsp olive oil
few knobs of butter
200g baby onions, peeled and roots trimmed
1 tsp caster sugar

TO SERVE:
about ½ head Savoy cabbage, cored and shredded
50g trompette de la mort (or other wild mushrooms), cleaned
1 tbsp olive oil
few knobs of butter
turnip purée (see page 250)
olive oil, to drizzle

FOR THE OSSO BUCCO, season the veal pieces and heat a wide pan or casserole. Add half the olive oil and brown the veal for 2 minutes on each side. Transfer to a plate. Add a little more oil to the pan and tip in the chopped vegetables, garlic and herbs. Fry for 4–6 minutes until the vegetables are soft. Add the tomato purée and stir for 2 minutes. Pour in the wine, scraping the bottom of the pan to deglaze. Let bubble until reduced by half. Add the veal stock and return the browned veal to the pan. Top up with a little water to cover the veal if necessary. Lay a piece of wet greaseproof paper on top of the veal to keep it submerged in the liquid. Turn the heat right down and leave to simmer very gently for 1½–2 hours until tender.

FOR THE POMMES BOULANGÈRE, preheat the oven to 200°C/Gas 6. Pour the chicken stock into a pan. Crush 2 garlic cloves and add to the stock with the herbs. Bring to the boil and boil for 2 minutes, then turn off the heat and leave to infuse for 10 minutes. Brush an ovenproof dish with olive oil. Finely chop the remaining 3 garlic cloves. Heat a little olive oil in a pan and gently sauté the garlic with the shallots for 4–6 minutes until softened and lightly coloured. In the meantime, peel and finely slice the potatoes using a mandolin.

LAYER THE POTATOES in the dish, overlapping the slices and sprinkling each layer with sautéed shallots, garlic and plenty of seasoning. Finish with a final layer of potatoes. Strain the infused stock and pour enough into the potato dish to come two-thirds of the way up the sides. Press down on the potatoes slightly, then dot the butter all over the top. Bake in the oven for 30–40 minutes or until the potatoes are golden brown on top and feel tender when pierced with a skewer. Keep warm.

FOR THE GLAZED BABY ONIONS, lower the oven setting to 180°C/Gas 4. Heat an ovenproof sauté pan, then add the olive oil and butter, followed by the baby onions. Shake the pan to coat the onions in the foaming butter, season well and sauté until the onions are lightly golden. Sprinkle with the sugar and toss well. Cover the pan with a piece of greaseproof paper and transfer to the oven. Roast for about 20–25 minutes, turning the onions every once in a while, until they have caramelised and are tender in the middle.

MEANWHILE, BLANCH THE SAVOY CABBAGE in boiling salted water for 1 minute, then drain and refresh in cold water. Drain and set aside.

REMOVE THE VEAL from the braising stock and set aside. Strain the stock through a fine sieve into a clean pan, pressing down on the vegetables with the back of a ladle to extract all the juices. Boil the stock until it has reduced down to a thick and syrupy sauce. Taste and adjust the seasoning.

WHEN READY TO SERVE, sauté the mushrooms with the olive oil and a knob of butter until softened. Reheat the veal in the sauce for a few minutes. Sauté the cabbage with a few knobs of butter until just tender. Place a round metal cutter on each warm plate and spoon in a layer of cabbage. Arrange the mushrooms in a circle around the plate. Place little dollops of turnip purée at intervals and top with the glazed baby onions. Remove the cutters and place the veal on top of the cabbage. Drizzle the reduced braising stock over the veal and drizzle a little olive oil around the plates. Slice the pomme boulangère into portions and serve on the side.

Risotto of ceps with spring onions, grated truffle and parmesan

THIS IS AN IDEAL MAIN COURSE FOR VEGETARIANS THAT CAN ALSO BE SERVED IN SMALLER PORTIONS AS A STARTER. RATHER THAN MAKE RISOTTO THE LABORIOUS, TRADITIONAL WAY, I BLANCH MY RICE IN ADVANCE, WHICH HALVES THE LAST-MINUTE COOKING TIME. THE RESULT IS JUST AS DELICIOUSLY RICH AND CREAMY, PROVIDED YOU USE A GOOD RISOTTO RICE. *[Illustrated on page 89]*

Serves 4 as a main course

SAUTÉED CEPS:
250g fresh ceps, cleaned
2 tbsp olive oil, plus extra to brush
sea salt and black pepper
few knobs of butter

RISOTTO:
200g risotto rice (such as carnaroli or vialone nano)
about 600ml vegetable stock (see page 247)
10g dried ceps (or porcini), rinsed
4 tbsp olive oil
2 banana shallots, peeled and finely chopped
100ml dry white wine
2 tbsp mascarpone
2 tbsp freshly grated parmesan
2 spring onions (green part only), finely chopped
20g butter

TO SERVE:
fresh truffle slices, to garnish
few parsley crisps (see page 248)
truffle-infused olive oil, to drizzle

HALVE 2 LARGE CEPS. Chop the rest and set all the mushrooms aside until ready to cook.

FOR THE RISOTTO, bring a large pan of salted water to the boil. Add the rice and blanch the grains for 5 minutes. Drain well and spread out on a lightly oiled tray. Let cool, then cover with cling film and set aside until ready to cook and serve. (If preparing several hours ahead, refrigerate.)

PUT THE STOCK in another saucepan with the dried ceps. Bring to the boil, then turn off the heat and leave to infuse for 10–15 minutes. Strain the stock and return to the pan. (You could use the ceps for another dish.)

WHEN READY TO COOK, heat 2 tbsp olive oil a saucepan and add the shallots. Stir over a medium heat for 3–4 minutes until beginning to soften. Tip in the rice and cook, stirring, for 1–2 minutes, then pour in the wine. Let bubble until almost totally reduced, then add a third of the infused stock. Stir occasionally until the rice has absorbed almost all the stock. Add another third of the stock and cook, stirring from time to time, again until the liquid is nearly all absorbed. Pour in half of the remaining stock, stir and simmer until absorbed. Now taste the rice to see if it is al dente. Add a splash more stock if the grains are still a little chalky. Remove the pan from the heat.

HEAT A GRIDDLE PAN until hot. Brush the ceps with a little olive oil and season well. Put the halved ceps on the griddle and cook for 4–5 minutes on both sides until nicely charred and cooked through. Heat the rest of the oil in a large frying pan and add the chopped ceps with a few knobs of butter. Season well and sauté over a high heat for 3–4 minutes until lightly browned.

RETURN THE RISOTTO to a gentle heat and add a little more stock. Stir in the sautéed ceps, then the mascarpone, parmesan, spring onions and finally the butter. Taste and adjust the seasoning.

DIVIDE THE RISOTTO among warm bowls and top each one with a griddled cep half. Garnish with the truffle slices and parsley crisps. Drizzle over a little truffle-infused oil and serve immediately.

DESSERTS

Caramelised pear tatin with
gorgonzola ice cream and
walnut cream

[Recipe on page 208]

Caramelised apple tarte tatin
with vanilla ice cream

[Recipe on page 210]

Carrot and white chocolate fondant
with dark chocolate sorbet

[Recipe on page 212]

Toffee soufflé
with banana and lime ice cream

[Recipe on page 214]

Lemon meringue
with marinated strawberries

[Recipe on page 216]

Plum crumble tart
with almond frangipane

[Recipe on page 218]

Raspberry compote
with tarragon cream

[Recipe on page 220]

Pineapple ravioli with mango filling,
berries and mint sorbet

[Recipe on page 222]

Pineapple and chilli soup
with fromage frais foam

[Recipe on page 224]

Sablé breton with raspberries, vanilla
cream and vanilla ice cream

[Recipe on page 226]

Tiramisu with coffee granita

[Recipe on page 228]

Raspberry, lemon and basil
millefeuille with milk ice cream

[Recipe on page 230]

Palet d'or with chocolate and
hazelnut ice cream and
passion fruit cream

[Recipe on page 232]

Slow-baked quince with crème
catalan, Pedro Ximenez gelée and
acacia honey granita

[Recipe on page 234]

Chocolate parfait with passion fruit
and guava coulis

[Recipe on page 236]

Bitter chocolate mousse with coffee
granita and light ginger cream

[Recipe on page 238]

Apple parfait with honeycomb, bitter
chocolate and champagne foam

[Recipe on page 241]

Caramelised pear tatin with gorgonzola ice cream and walnut

cream IN THE RESTAURANT WE MAKE INDIVIDUAL TATINS IN SMALL SHALLOW PANS, BUT YOU CAN

MAKE A LARGE TART USING A SAUTÉ PAN OR A 20–21CM TATIN TIN INSTEAD. GORGONZOLA ICE CREAM IS

AN IDEAL PARTNER, BUT YOU CAN SERVE A SIMPLE VANILLA ICE CREAM IF YOU PREFER. *[Illustrated on page 93]*

Serves 6

PEAR TATIN:
500g ready-made puff pastry
6 Williams pears
150g unsalted butter
150g caster sugar

GORGONZOLA ICE CREAM:
250ml milk
250ml double cream
6 egg yolks
100g caster sugar
125g gorgonzola, crumbled

WALNUT CREAM:
250ml double cream
25g caster sugar
50g skinned and lightly toasted walnuts, chopped

TO SERVE:
reduced light caramel, to drizzle (optional)
6 dried pear slices (see page 251), optional

FIRST, MAKE THE ICE CREAM. Put the milk and cream into a saucepan and slowly bring to the boil. Meanwhile, beat the egg yolks and sugar together in a large bowl. As the creamy milk begins to boil, slowly pour it onto the yolk and sugar mix, whisking continuously. Strain through a fine sieve into a clean pan.

RETURN TO A LOW HEAT and stir constantly with a wooden spoon until slightly thickened, to form a light custard. Add the crumbled cheese and stir until it melts and the custard is smooth. Leave to cool completely, stirring every once in a while to prevent a skin forming on the surface. Pour into an ice cream machine and churn until almost firm. Transfer the ice cream to a shallow container and freeze for a few hours or overnight until firm.

FOR THE WALNUT CREAM, put the cream and sugar in a saucepan and stir over a low heat until the sugar has dissolved, then increase the heat. When the liquid is almost boiling, take off the heat and tip in the walnuts. Leave to infuse and cool slightly for 10 minutes. Whiz the creamy walnut infusion in a blender until smooth, then pass through a fine sieve into a bowl, pressing down on the pulp in the sieve with the back of a spoon. Using an electric beater, whip the cream to soft peaks, then cover and chill until ready to serve.

FOR THE PEAR TATINS, have ready six 9cm ovenproof pans. Peel and halve the pears, then scoop out the cores, using a melon baller. Lay the pear halves out on a tray lined with kitchen paper and pat with more kitchen paper. Leave to dry uncovered for a few hours, or chill overnight if possible; it won't matter if they discolour because they'll be coated in caramel anyway.

ROLL OUT THE PUFF PASTRY thinly on a lightly floured surface. Cut 6 rounds (slightly larger than the diameter of the pans), using an 11–12cm plate as a guide. Lay the pastry discs on a tray lined with baking parchment. Cover and chill while you prepare the pears and caramel.

CUT THE BUTTER INTO THIN SLICES, scatter over the bottom of the ovenproof pans and sprinkle over the sugar. Place the pans over a medium heat until the butter and sugar have melted and formed a light caramel. Add the pears and cook for about 8 minutes until the caramel turns deep amber and the pears are golden brown. Remove from the heat and leave to cool.

REARRANGE THE PEARS as necessary, so they are cut side up in the pans. Carefully drape the puff pastry discs over the pears and tuck the edges down the side of the pan. (At this stage, the tatins can be kept chilled for a few hours, ready for baking half an hour before serving.)

WHEN READY TO COOK, preheat the oven to 200°C/Gas 6. Place the tatin pans in the oven and bake for 20–25 minutes until the pastry is golden brown and crisp. Leave to cool slightly.

TO SERVE, drizzle individual serving plates decoratively with a little reduced caramel if you like. Carefully invert the pans and turn out the pear tatins onto the plates. Place a scoop of gorgonzola ice cream and a spoonful of walnut cream on each plate and decorate with dried pear slices if using. Serve at once.

Caramelised apple tarte tatin with vanilla ice cream THIS ELEGANT

DESSERT IS DESIGNED TO SERVE TWO, BUT YOU CAN EASILY MAKE AN EXTRA TATIN OR TWO TO SERVE

MORE; THERE IS ENOUGH ICE CREAM FOR 5–6 PORTIONS. VANILLA PODS DUSTED WITH ICING SUGAR

PROVIDE THE PERFECT FINISHING TOUCH – DRY THE EMPTY PODS AFTER YOU HAVE MADE THE ICE

CREAM TO USE FOR THE DECORATION. *[Illustrated on page 95]*

Serves 2

APPLE TATIN:
3 large crisp dessert apples (such as Pink Lady)
250g ready-made puff pastry
50g cold unsalted butter
50g caster sugar

VANILLA ICE CREAM:
250ml double cream
250ml milk
2 vanilla pods, split
6 egg yolks
100g caster sugar

TO SERVE:
2–3 vanilla pods (seeds removed), sliced lengthways
icing sugar, to dust

TO PREPARE THE APPLES, peel, core and quarter them, then lay out on a tray lined with kitchen paper. Leave to dry uncovered for 2–3 hours, or preferably chill overnight. Don't worry if they turn brown; they will be coated in caramel.

NEXT, MAKE THE ICE CREAM. Pour the double cream and milk into a pan. Scrape out the seeds from the vanilla pods and add them to the pan with the empty pods. Slowly bring to the boil. Meanwhile, beat the egg yolks and sugar together in a large bowl. As the creamy milk begins to boil, slowly pour it onto the yolk and sugar mix, whisking all the time. Strain through a fine sieve into a clean pan.

STIR THE CUSTARD over a low heat with a wooden spoon until it thickens enough to lightly coat the back of the spoon. Leave to cool completely, stirring every once in a while to prevent a skin forming. Pass the cooled custard through a fine sieve, removing the pods. Pour into an ice cream machine and churn until thick and smooth. Transfer the ice cream to a plastic container and freeze for a few hours or overnight until firm.

FOR THE TARTE TATIN, have ready a 20cm shallow ovenproof pan. Roll out the pastry thinly on a lightly floured surface and cut out a 24cm round, using a similar-sized plate as a guide. Lift onto a baking sheet and chill while you prepare the filling.

CUT THE BUTTER INTO THIN SLICES and scatter over the bottom of a 20cm ovenproof pan. Sprinkle over the sugar. Arrange the apple quarters neatly around the pan with one in the middle. Place over a medium heat until the butter and sugar have melted and formed a light caramel. Carefully shake the pan from time to time to ensure that the apples are well coated with the caramel and are evenly brown. Leave to cool slightly.

WHEN READY TO COOK, preheat the oven to 200°C/Gas 6. Drape the pastry over the apples and carefully tuck the edges down the sides of the pan. Place the pan in the hot oven and bake for 15 minutes. Lower the oven setting to 180°C/Gas 4 and bake for a further 15–20 minutes until the pastry is golden brown and crisp. Leave to cool.

TO SERVE, dust the sliced vanilla pods liberally with icing sugar, shaking off excess. Turn out the tarte tatin onto a serving plate, top with the sugar-dusted vanilla and serve with scoops of vanilla ice cream.

Carrot and white chocolate fondant with dark chocolate sorbet

THE COMBINATION OF FLAVOURS IN THESE PUDDINGS IS TRULY DELICIOUS. IF YOU DO NOT HAVE THE

CYLINDRICAL MOULDS DESCRIBED, USE METAL PANNACOTTA OR DARIOLE MOULDS, MAKING SURE THAT

THE CENTRES ARE WELL CONTAINED WITHIN THE CAKE BATTER, OTHERWISE THE PUDDINGS WILL NOT

HOLD UP. PREPARE THE SORBET, CARROT PURÉE AND CENTRES WELL IN ADVANCE. *[Illustrated on page 98]*

Serves about 10–12

CARROT PURÉE:
500g large Chantenay carrots, trimmed and peeled
750ml fresh carrot juice (prepared with a juicer, or from a health food store)

SOFT CENTRES:
160ml double cream
30g white chocolate

CAKE BATTER:
80g unsalted butter, plus extra for brushing
75g good-quality white chocolate
110g reduced carrot purée (see recipe)
5 large egg yolks
65g ground almonds
pinch of ground cinnamon
50g rice flour
30g walnuts, finely chopped
120g egg whites (about 3 large eggs)
135g caster sugar

DARK CHOCOLATE SORBET:
200g dark, bitter chocolate (approx 75% cocoa solids)
150ml whipping cream
100g caster sugar
400ml water

FIRST, MAKE THE SORBET. Chop the dark chocolate and place in a heatproof bowl. Combine the cream, sugar and water in a saucepan and stir over a low heat until the sugar has dissolved. Bring to the boil and immediately pour onto the chocolate, stirring constantly. Continue to stir until the mixture is smooth, then pass through a fine sieve into a bowl and leave to cool completely. Pour into an ice cream machine and churn until almost firm. Transfer to a suitable container and freeze for a few hours or overnight until firm.

TO MAKE THE CARROT PURÉE, roughly chop the carrots and place in a saucepan with the carrot juice. Cover with a piece of wet greaseproof paper and bring to the boil. Cook for 15–20 minutes or until the carrots are very soft and the liquid has reduced by half. Transfer the carrots and juice to a blender and whiz to a fine, smooth purée; it should be quite firm, not runny. Measure out 300g of the purée and set aside for the soft molten centres.

PUT THE REMAINING CARROT PURÉE in a clean pan and cook over a medium heat for another 15–20 minutes, stirring frequently, to reduce and dry out a little. Leave to cool. Measure 110g reduced carrot purée for the cake mixture and set aside. (Use any remaining purée for another dish.)

TO PREPARE THE SOFT CENTRES, put the cream into a saucepan and slowly bring to the boil. Meanwhile, chop the white chocolate into small pieces and put into a heatproof bowl. As soon as the cream begins to boil, remove from the heat and pour onto the white chocolate, stirring continuously until the mixture is smooth. Cool slightly, then mix in the reserved 300g carrot purée. Pour the mixture into a shallow plastic container and freeze for a few hours or overnight until firm.

FOR THE CAKE, preheat the oven to 180°C/Gas 4. Line the bases of 10–12 straight-sided cylindrical moulds, about 4cm in diameter and 6cm in height, with baking parchment discs. Brush these and the sides of the moulds with soft butter. Stand the prepared moulds on a baking tray and set aside. Remove the frozen carrot and white chocolate mixture from the freezer and set aside to soften slightly in a cool part of the kitchen while you make the cake batter.

CHOP THE WHITE CHOCOLATE and place in a heatproof bowl with the butter. Melt slowly over a pan of barely simmering water. Stir until the mixture is smooth, then remove from the heat. Gradually add the 110g reduced carrot purée, stirring until smooth, then incorporate the egg yolks. Mix together the ground almonds, cinnamon, rice flour and chopped walnuts, then fold into the carrot mixture.

IN A CLEAN, DRY BOWL, whisk the egg whites with an electric mixer to soft peaks. Whisk in the sugar, a tablespoon at a time, and continue to whisk until the meringue is firm and shiny. Carefully fold into the carrot batter.

WORKING FAST, use a round metal cutter (about 1.5–2cm in diameter and 3cm deep) to stamp out little cylinders from the frozen carrot and white chocolate centres. Put 1–2 tbsp of cake batter into each prepared mould, then carefully lower a carrot and white chocolate cylinder into the centre of each mould. Spoon over another 1–2 tbsp of cake batter to cover the cylinders and fill the moulds. Bake for 20–25 minutes until the tops of the fondants are golden brown. (Remove from the oven at once if the tops look as though they are about to burst open to reveal the filling.)

HOLDING EACH MOULD with a cloth to protect your hands, run a small, thin knife around the side of the fondant, then invert onto a serving plate and remove the mould. Place a quenelle of chocolate sorbet alongside and serve straight away.

Toffee soufflé with banana and lime ice cream

A SOUFFLÉ NEVER FAILS TO IMPRESS. JUST MAKE SURE YOU HAVE EVERYTHING READY AND WAITING THE MOMENT YOU TAKE THE DISHES FROM THE OVEN – SERVING PLATES, ICE CREAM AND GUESTS. MAKE THE SOUFFLÉ BASE, NOUGATINE AND ICE CREAM WELL AHEAD, READY TO WHIP UP THE MERINGUE AND FOLD IT INTO THE SOUFFLÉ BASE AT THE LAST MINUTE. *[Illustrated on page 99]*

Serves about 8

SOUFFLÉ BASE:
40g butter, softened to room temperature,
  plus extra for brushing
60g plain flour
pinch of fine sea salt
3 large egg yolks
150ml milk
85g caster sugar

MERINGUE:
8 large egg whites
75g caster sugar

NOUGATINE:
150g caster sugar
30g toasted flaked almonds

BANANA AND LIME ICE CREAM:
500ml whole milk
500ml double cream
1 vanilla pod, split (optional)
8 large egg yolks
350g caster sugar
3 medium bananas
60ml crème de banane liqueur
100ml lime juice (2–3 limes)

FOR THE SOUFFLÉ BASE, in a large bowl, beat 15g butter with the flour, salt and egg yolks to a thick paste. Heat the milk in a saucepan to just below the boil, then gradually beat into the paste a little at a time until the mixture is smooth. Pass through a fine sieve back into the pan, pushing it through with the back of a spoon. Stir over a low heat for about 3 minutes until the mixture is very thick. Transfer to a food processor and whiz until very smooth. Leave in the processor while you make the toffee.

MELT THE 85G SUGAR in a dry heavy-based pan over a high heat, swirling the pan as the sugar begins to melt at the edges. When it forms a dark caramel, take the pan off the heat and carefully add the remaining butter, shaking the pan to mix the caramel with the butter.

WITH THE MOTOR RUNNING, slowly pour the toffee onto the soufflé base in the processor, blending until well mixed. Transfer to a large bowl and allow to cool if not using immediately. (The soufflé base can be kept chilled for 2–3 days.)

FOR THE NOUGATINE, melt the sugar in a dry heavy-based pan, swirling the pan as the sugar melts and caramelises. When it reaches a terracotta colour, mix in the almonds. Immediately pour onto a non-stick baking tray (or silicone-lined baking sheet). Tilt the tray to level the nut caramel and leave to cool for about 15 minutes until it is firm and brittle.

BREAK UP THE NOUGATINE, then finely chop with a strong knife. Store in an airtight container until ready to use.

FOR THE BANANA ICE CREAM, make the crème anglaise. Pour the milk and cream into a heavy-based pan. If using vanilla, scrape the seeds into the creamy milk and add the pod too. Slowly bring to the boil. Meanwhile, beat the egg yolks and 250g of the sugar together in a large bowl. As it is about to boil, slowly pour the creamy milk onto the eggs and sugar, whisking continuously. Strain through a fine sieve into a clean pan and stir with a wooden spoon over a low heat until the crème anglaise has thickened enough to lightly coat the back of a wooden spoon. Pour into a bowl and cool quickly over a bowl of iced water, stirring occasionally to prevent a skin forming.

FINELY PURÉE TWO BANANAS in a blender until smooth (you need 200g purée); roughly chop the other banana. Heat the remaining 100g sugar in a non-stick frying pan until melted and turned to a light caramel. Add the chopped banana and toss over a high heat to caramelise. Take off the heat and stir in the banana purée, crème de banane and lime juice. Return to the heat and stir until the mixture is smooth. Tip into the crème anglaise and use a hand-held stick blender to combine the mixtures. Transfer to an ice cream machine and churn until almost firm. Scoop into a shallow container and freeze until firm.

HALF AN HOUR BEFORE SERVING, warm up the soufflé base by placing the bowl in a large pan half-filled with warm water for about 20–25 minutes; this will make it easier to work with.

PREHEAT THE OVEN to 190°C/Gas 5. Brush eight 300ml individual soufflé dishes (about 6.5cm deep and 9.5cm in diameter) with soft butter. Chill until firm, then brush again with another layer of butter. Dust with chopped nougatine and shake out any excess; reserve. Place a heavy baking sheet in the oven to heat up.

FOR THE MERINGUE, whisk the egg whites in a clean, dry bowl until stiff, then whisk in the sugar, a tablespoonful at a time, until fully incorporated and the meringue holds soft peaks. Using a large metal spoon, fold the meringue into the soufflé base. Spoon the mixture into the prepared dishes until almost full. Run the knife around the top edge of the dishes, then sprinkle any remaining crushed nougatine on top. Stand the dishes on the hot baking sheet and bake for about 10 minutes. The soufflés are ready when they are golden brown and feel a little springy when lightly pressed. (If your oven is too hot and the soufflés look as though they are about to crack in the middle, take them out.)

STAND THE SOUFFLÉ DISHES on individual serving plates with a little dish of banana and lime ice cream on the side. Serve immediately.

Lemon meringue with marinated strawberries AT THE RESTAURANT, WE

BAKE MERINGUES IN A STEAM OVEN TO GET A SOFT CENTRE. HERE THEY ARE PARTLY COOKED IN THE

MICROWAVE, THEN BAKED BRIEFLY IN A HOT OVEN TO ACHIEVE A SIMILAR RESULT. BLACK PEPPER AND

SESAME TUILES ARE PERFECT WITH THIS DESSERT, BUT YOU CAN SERVE IT WITH ANY CRISP DESSERT

BISCUITS. *[Illustrated on page 100]*

Serves 8–10

LEMON MERINGUE:
100g egg whites (2–3 large eggs)
75g caster sugar
finely grated zest of 2 lemons
icing sugar, to dust

STRAWBERRY SORBET:
500g ripe strawberries, hulled
juice of 1 large lemon
200g caster sugar
200ml water
1½ tbsp liquid glucose

BLACK PEPPER AND SESAME TUILES:
75g icing sugar
20ml cold water
25g plain flour
50g lightly salted butter, melted
30g white sesame seeds
cracked black pepper, to sprinkle

VANILLA OIL:
seeds from ½ vanilla pod
4 tbsp olive oil

TO SERVE:
250g strawberries (ideally including some fraises des bois), hulled and larger ones halved
good-quality aged balsamic vinegar, to drizzle
handful of small basil leaves

FIRST, MAKE THE SORBET. Put the strawberries and lemon juice into a food processor and whiz to a smooth purée. Tip into a saucepan, bring to the boil and let bubble until reduced by half. Allow to cool slightly, then rub the purée through a fine sieve to remove the seeds. Leave the purée to cool completely.

PUT THE SUGAR AND WATER in a heavy-based saucepan. Add the liquid glucose and heat gently until the sugar has dissolved. Increase the heat and boil the syrup for 5 minutes until slightly thickened. Cool completely, then mix with the strawberry purée. Pour the mixture into an ice cream machine and churn until almost firm. Transfer to a suitable container and freeze until firm.

TO MAKE THE TUILES, preheat the oven to 180°C/Gas 4 and line a flat baking sheet with a silicone liner (such as silpat or bake-o-glide). Sift the icing sugar into a bowl, add the water and stir until well blended. Mix in the flour, then stir in the melted butter. Finally, stir in the sesame seeds.

SPREAD 1–2 TBSP OF THE BATTER on the prepared baking sheet. Place a large piece of baking parchment on top and roll out the batter thinly using a rolling pin. Carefully peel off the parchment and sprinkle over the black pepper. Bake for 6–8 minutes until golden brown. Leave to cool for 1 minute only.

WHILE THE TUILE IS STILL WARM and pliable, cut it into long strips, about 1.5cm wide and 9cm long. If it becomes too brittle to cut, return to the oven for a minute to soften slightly. The tuiles will crisp up once cooled. Repeat, using the rest of the batter, to make more tuiles. Store in an airtight container, separating the layers with baking parchment, until ready to serve.

FOR THE LEMON MERINGUE, preheat the oven to 200°C/Gas 6. Line a non-metal tray (suitable to go in a microwave) with baking parchment. Put the egg whites into a large clean bowl (or the bowl of an electric mixer). Beat slowly to begin with, then increase the speed to high and beat continuously until the egg whites form soft peaks. Gradually whisk in the sugar, a tablespoonful at a time, until fully incorporated and the meringue is smooth and glossy. Do not over-whisk; stop if the meringue begins to look grainy around the edges. Finally, carefully fold in the grated lemon zest.

PIPE THE MERINGUE IN BATCHES. Spoon into a disposable piping bag and cut off the tip to create an opening about 3.5cm in diameter. Pipe thick straight lines, about 9–10cm in length onto the lined tray. Gently pat down the peaked ends of each meringue with a wet finger. Microwave on the highest setting for 20 seconds. Remove and slide the baking parchment onto a baking sheet.

DUST THE MERINGUES heavily with icing sugar, then bake in the oven for about 3 minutes until lightly golden. The meringues should feel a little crisp on the outside where the sugar has caramelised, with a soft, slightly mallowy centre.

FOR THE VANILLA OIL, mix the vanilla seeds with the olive oil.

WHEN READY TO SERVE, trim the ends of the meringues diagonally, then use a palette knife to carefully lift them onto individual serving plates. Arrange the strawberries on both sides and drizzle with a little balsamic vinegar. Scatter the basil leaves around the berries and drizzle a little vanilla oil around each plate. Add a scoop of strawberry sorbet and a tuile to each plate and serve immediately, with the rest of the tuiles handed around separately.

Plum crumble tart with almond frangipane
MAKE ALL THE DIFFERENT COMPONENTS OF THIS DESSERT A DAY IN ADVANCE, READY TO ASSEMBLE AND BAKE A FEW HOURS BEFORE SERVING. I LOVE THIS DRAMATIC PRESENTATION, BUT YOU COULD SIMPLY SPOON THE PLUM SAUCE AROUND THE TARTS TO SAVE TIME. *[Illustrated on page 101]*

Makes about 10

PASTRY:
225g plain flour
pinch of fine sea salt
1 tsp caster sugar
140g unsalted butter, diced
1 medium egg yolk, beaten with 2 ½ tbsp water

FRANGIPANE:
75g unsalted butter, softened to room temperature
75g caster sugar
1 large egg, lightly beaten
75g finely ground almonds (or almond powder)

PLUM FILLING AND SAUCE:
12 firm (slightly under-ripe) plums
1 litre stock syrup (see page 251)

PLUM PURÉE:
3 plums
2 tbsp caster sugar

CRUMBLE:
45g plain flour
pinch of fine sea salt
40g unsalted butter, diced
35g caster sugar
45g finely ground almonds

TO ASSEMBLE:
icing sugar, to dust
plain dark chocolate, melted, to decorate

TO SERVE:
clotted cream or vanilla ice cream (see page 251)

FOR THE PASTRY, sift the flour and salt into a bowl and stir in the sugar. Put into a food processor along with the butter and whiz until the mixture resembles coarse crumbs. Add the beaten egg and pulse for a few seconds until the mixture comes together. Tip onto a lightly floured surface, gather into a ball and knead for a minute until smooth; avoid overworking the dough. Wrap in cling film and leave to rest in the fridge for 30 minutes before rolling out.

FOR THE FRANGIPANE, beat the butter and sugar together in a bowl until pale and creamy. Incorporate the egg and finally the ground almonds. Cover the bowl with cling film and set aside.

FOR THE PLUM FILLING, halve and stone 8 plums, then cut into wedges. Place in a small saucepan with the stock syrup over a low heat and gently poach the plums for 6–8 minutes until softened but still holding their shape. With a slotted spoon, transfer to a bowl and leave to cool. Reserve the syrup.

FOR THE SAUCE, halve and stone the other 4 plums and cut into wedges. Poach in the reserved stock syrup for 8–10 minutes until soft. Transfer to a blender with 2–3 tbsp of the poaching syrup and whiz to a smooth purée. Push the purée through a fine sieve into a bowl and add a little more of the syrup if the sauce is too thick. Cool, then pour into a plastic squeezy bottle. Reserve the rest of the poaching syrup.

FOR THE PLUM PURÉE, halve, stone and roughly chop the plums. Toss with the sugar and place in a large non-stick frying pan. Cook over a medium heat until the plums are softened and any juices have been cooked off. If the pan looks too dry and the sugar begins to caramelise, add 1–2 tbsp of the poaching syrup. When soft, tip the plums into a blender and whiz to a smooth purée. Transfer to a bowl and leave to cool.

PREHEAT THE OVEN to 200°C/Gas 6. Roll out the pastry on a lightly floured surface and use to line 8cm tartlet tins, preferably with removable bases. Chill for 20 minutes. Line the tartlet cases with greaseproof paper and baking beans and bake for 15 minutes. Remove the beans and paper and return to the oven for 5 minutes. Cool slightly, then spread a thin layer of frangipane over the base of each tartlet case. Bake for 8–10 minutes or until the frangipane is lightly golden.

MEANWHILE, MAKE THE CRUMBLE. Put the flour, salt and butter in a food processor and blend briefly until the mixture looks like fine crumbs. Add the sugar and ground almonds and pulse for a few seconds to mix. Don't overprocess; the mixture needs to be crumbly and uneven in texture.

SPREAD A LITTLE PLUM PURÉE in each tart case. Arrange 5–6 poached plum segments in an overlapping circle on top, with the skins facing outwards.

SPRINKLE A LITTLE CRUMBLE in the centre of each tart and dust lightly with icing sugar. Bake for 5 minutes until the crumble topping is golden. Leave to cool.

TO SERVE, pipe a flower outline on each serving plate using the melted chocolate. Fill with the plum sauce, using the back of a teaspoon to help spread the sauce. Place the plum tart in the centre. Serve with clotted cream or vanilla ice cream.

Raspberry compote with tarragon cream THESE LITTLE LIGHT CUSTARD POTS ARE EASY TO PREPARE. MAKE THE RASPBERRY COMPOTE AND TARRAGON CREAM SEVERAL HOURS IN ADVANCE AND KEEP THEM CHILLED, READY TO ASSEMBLE AND SERVE. *[Illustrated on page 103]*

Serves 6–8

RASPBERRY COMPOTE:
250g raspberries
50g caster sugar

TARRAGON CREAM:
200ml double cream
200ml whole milk
20g tarragon leaves, roughly chopped
75g caster sugar, plus an extra 1 tbsp
7 large egg yolks

TO SERVE:
cocoa powder, to dust

FOR THE RASPBERRY COMPOTE, put the raspberries and sugar in a non-stick pan and cook over a high heat for a few minutes, shaking the pan, until the fruit has broken down and the juices are reduced and syrupy. Tip into a bowl and leave to cool completely.

SPOON A THIN LAYER of raspberry compote into 6 to 8 small serving glasses (or individual glass pots as we do in the restaurant), reserving about 2 tbsp for serving. Cover the pots with cling film and chill.

FOR THE TARRAGON CREAM, heat the cream, milk and chopped tarragon in a saucepan with 1 tbsp sugar. As soon as the liquid starts to boil, remove the pan from the heat and set aside to infuse for 15–20 minutes.

BEAT THE EGG YOLKS AND SUGAR together in a large bowl until light and creamy, then pour in the strained cream mixture, strring until smooth.

POUR THE CREAMY MIXTURE into a large heavy-based saucepan and place over a low heat. Stir continuously with a wooden spoon until the custard is thick enough to lightly coat the back of the spoon. Strain the tarragon cream into a clean bowl and discard the tarragon. Leave to cool, stirring occasionally to prevent a skin forming on the surface. Cover with cling film and chill for a few hours or overnight to allow the custard to firm up slightly.

TO SERVE, spoon the tarragon cream into the serving glasses to form a thick layer over the raspberry compote. Dust the surface with cocoa powder, then carefully drop a scant teaspoonful of the reserved raspberry compote on top. Serve immediately.

Pineapple ravioli with mango filling, berries and mint sorbet

THIS FRUITY DESSERT IS WONDERFULLY REFRESHING, ESPECIALLY WHEN SERVED WITH A FRESH MINT SORBET, AS WE DO IN THE RESTAURANT. FOR A MORE INTENSE FLAVOUR WE FOLD REDUCED MANGO PURÉE THROUGH THE RAVIOLI FILLING, BUT THIS IS NOT ESSENTIAL. STEEP THE PINEAPPLE SLICES IN THE SYRUP OVERNIGHT AND PREPARE THE MINT SORBET 4–6 HOURS AHEAD. *[Illustrated on page 104]*

Serves 6–8

PINEAPPLE RAVIOLI :
200ml stock syrup (see page 251)
200ml water
30ml light rum
juice of 1/2 lemon
1 vanilla pod, split and seeds removed
1 large, ripe pineapple

MANGO FILLING:
1 large mango
50g crème fraîche
50g mascarpone
seeds from 1/2 vanilla pod
50g mango purée
2–3 tbsp sifted icing sugar (optional)

MINT SORBET:
250ml lemon juice (from about 6 lemons)
250ml stock syrup (see page 251)
350ml water
large bunch of mint, leaves only
125ml crème de menthe

TO SERVE:
about 100g mixed berries (such as blueberries, raspberries, baby strawberries and raspberries)
few candied orange peel (optional)
few crystallised mint leaves (optional)

FOR THE PINEAPPLE RAVIOLI, pour the stock syrup and water into a medium saucepan and add the rum, lemon juice and vanilla pod. Bring to the boil and let bubble for 5 minutes until reduced slightly, then transfer to a large bowl and leave to cool.

TO PREPARE THE PINEAPPLE, cut off the top and base, then stand the fruit upright on the board and slice away the skin, following the natural curve of the fruit. Prise out any remaining 'eyes' with the tip of a sharp knife. Now turn the pineapple on its side and cut 16–24 very thin slices, using a long, serrated knife. Lay the pineapple slices in the cooled syrup as you cut them, ensuring that each slice is well coated before adding another. Cover the bowl with cling film and leave to macerate in the fridge overnight, so the pineapple slices soften.

TO MAKE THE MINT SORBET, put the lemon juice, stock syrup, water and mint into a saucepan and bring to the boil. Boil for 2–3 minutes, then take off the heat and set aside to infuse and cool completely. Pour through a fine sieve into a bowl to strain out the mint leaves. Stir the crème de menthe into the infused syrup, then pour into an ice cream maker and churn until almost firm. Transfer to a plastic container and freeze. (For the best texture, serve this sorbet the same day.)

FOR THE MANGO FILLING, peel the fruit and cut the flesh away from the stone, then chop into 5mm cubes. Mix the crème fraîche, mascarpone and vanilla seeds together in a bowl, then stir in the mango purée. Fold through the chopped mango and sweeten with icing sugar to taste. Chill until ready to serve.

WHEN READY TO SERVE, drain the pineapple slices, reserving the liquor. To thicken this if required, pour into a small pan and boil for 5–7 minutes until reduced and syrupy.

TO ASSEMBLE, pat each pineapple slice with kitchen paper, then place the smallest 6 slices on individual serving plates. Using a small ice cream scoop, shape the mango filling into balls and place one on the centre of each pineapple base. Drape one or two larger pineapple slices over the top and press down the sides slightly to mould around the filling. Arrange the berries around the plates. If using, top each blueberry with a sliver of candied orange peel and each raspberry with a crystallised mint leaf. Drizzle over a little pineapple syrup and serve.

Pineapple and chilli soup with fromage frais foam I LOVE THIS

FRIVOLOUS DESSERT WITH ITS CONTRASTING LAYERS OF FLAVOURS – TANGY PINEAPPLE, LIGHT LEMONY

FROMAGE FRAIS AND FLAVOUR BURSTS OF CHILLI AND STARDUST CANDY. PREPARE THE PINEAPPLE SOUP

AND THE CHILLI SYRUP WELL IN ADVANCE. *[Illustrated on page 105]*

Serves 4–6

PINEAPPLE SOUP:
1 large, ripe pineapple
50g caster sugar, or to taste
75ml Champagne or sparkling white wine
splash of pineapple juice, to taste

CHILLI SYRUP (OPTIONAL):
50ml stock syrup (see page 251)
pinch of dried chilli flakes

FROMAGE FRAIS FOAM:
100g fromage frais
125ml whole milk
150ml stock syrup (see page 251)
juice of 2 lemons
2 sheets of leaf gelatine

TO SERVE:
few pinches of stardust candy (optional)
1 dried chilli, deseeded and very finely chopped

TO PREPARE THE PINEAPPLE, cut off the top and base, then stand the fruit upright on the board and slice away the skin, following the natural curve of the fruit. Prise out any remaining 'eyes' with the tip of a sharp knife. Cut into quarters lengthways, remove the tough central core and roughly chop the flesh. Toss the pineapple chunks with the sugar. Place a large frying pan over a high heat, add the pineapple and toss for a few minutes until the chunks begin to soften and caramelise slightly.

TIP THE PINEAPPLE into a food processor or blender and whiz to a fine purée. Pass through a fine sieve into a bowl, pushing the pulp in the sieve with the back of a ladle to extract all the juice. Discard the pulp. Taste the strained juice and balance out the flavour with the Champagne and a splash of pineapple juice. Cover the bowl with cling film and chill until ready to serve.

FOR THE CHILLI SYRUP, if using, bring the sugar syrup to the boil, add a pinch of chilli flakes and turn off the heat. Let cool completely, then strain through a fine sieve and chill until ready to use.

FOR THE FROMAGE FRAIS FOAM, beat the fromage frais and milk together in a large bowl. Put the stock syrup and lemon juice in a saucepan, bring to the boil and let bubble for 5 minutes until slightly reduced.

MEANWHILE, SOAK THE GELATINE leaves in cold water to cover for a few minutes until softened. Take the lemon syrup off the heat. Drain the gelatine leaves and squeeze out excess water, then add to the hot lemon syrup, stirring to dissolve. Leave to cool slightly, for about 5 minutes, then whisk into the fromage frais mixture. Place the bowl over a larger bowl or pan filled with iced water. Whisk the mixture every now and then as it cools and starts to set. When it is softly set, cover the bowl with cling film and chill until ready to serve.

WHEN READY TO SERVE, half-fill 4 to 6 chilled tall glasses with the pineapple soup. If using, add a tiny drizzle of chilli syrup to each glass and drop in a large pinch of stardust candy if you like.

WHISK THE FROMAGE FRAIS FOAM with a balloon whisk or an electric beater until light and airy. (In the restaurant we use a soda siphon to make and apply the foam, but this method works too.)

SPOON THE FOAM into the glasses and sprinkle over a tiny pinch of dried chopped chilli. Pop a long, wide straw into each glass and serve.

Sablé breton with raspberries, vanilla cream and vanilla ice cream

THESE LITTLE SHORTBREADS HAVE A LOVELY, BUTTERY FLAVOUR – THE PERFECT BASE FOR STRAWBERRIES AND VANILLA CREAM. MAKE THE SABLÉ DOUGH AHEAD AND FREEZE IT IF YOU LIKE – CUT INTO DISCS AND BAKE FROM FROZEN, ALLOWING AN EXTRA FEW MINUTES. THE DESSERT IS QUICK TO ASSEMBLE IF YOU MAKE THE VANILLA CREAM AND RASPBERRY BUTTER SAUCE IN ADVANCE, TOO.

[Illustrated on page 107]

Serves 10–12

SABLÉ BRETON:
225g plain flour
pinch of fine sea salt
1 tbsp baking powder
160g salted butter, softened to room temperature, plus extra for brushing
160g caster sugar
4 large egg yolks, lightly beaten

VANILLA CREAM:
250ml whole milk
½ vanilla pod
55g caster sugar
3 medium egg yolks
20g cornflour
75–100ml double cream

RASPBERRY BUTTER SAUCE:
350g raspberries
4 tbsp stock syrup (see page 251)
75g unsalted butter, diced

TO ASSEMBLE:
melted plain dark chocolate, to decorate
150g raspberries
icing sugar, to dust
4 scoops of vanilla ice cream (see page 251)
plain dark chocolate rectangles (optional)
handful of sugar-coated pistachios (optional)
reduced stock syrup (see page 251), to drizzle

FOR THE SABLÉ BRETON, sift the flour, salt and baking powder together and set aside. Using an electric mixer, beat the butter until it is light and creamy. Add the sugar and continue to beat, scraping the bowl as necessary, until the mixture is light and fluffy. Beat in the egg yolks, a little at a time, until fully incorporated. Now using a large rubber spatula, fold in the sifted dry ingredients, taking care to avoid overworking the dough.

SHAPE THE DOUGH into a thick log, about 7–8cm in diameter, and wrap tightly in cling film. Chill for a few hours until firm. (The sablé dough can also be frozen for up to a month.)

TO MAKE THE VANILLA CREAM, pour the milk into a saucepan, scrape out the vanilla seeds and add these to the milk with the empty pod and 1 tbsp sugar. Slowly bring to the boil. Meanwhile, beat the remaining sugar and egg yolks together in a large bowl until creamy. Beat in the cornflour until the mixture is smooth. Just as the milk begins to scald, remove from the heat and gradually trickle onto the egg mixture, whisking continuously. When fully incorporated, pass through a fine sieve into a clean pan. Slowly stir the mixture over a low heat for 5 minutes or so, to cook out the cornflour and thicken the custard. Again, pass through a sieve into a large bowl. Leave to cool, stirring occasionally, to prevent a skin forming.

WHIP THE CREAM in another bowl to soft peaks, then fold into the cooled custard. Transfer to a large piping bag and refrigerate until ready to serve.

PREHEAT THE OVEN to 180°C/Gas 4. Lightly butter 10–12 metal pastry rings, 7–8cm in diameter, and place on a large baking sheet; alternatively use a 12-hole muffin tin. Unwrap the sablé dough log and slice it into 1.5cm discs. Put a disc in each pastry ring (or muffin mould) and bake for 8–10 minutes until pale golden in colour. Leave in the moulds for a few minutes, then transfer to a wire rack to cool completely. Store in an airtight container if not serving immediately.

FOR THE RASPBERRY BUTTER SAUCE, whiz the raspberries and stock syrup together in a blender, then rub the purée through a fine sieve into a small pan. Bring the raspberry purée to the boil and let bubble until reduced by about a third, to 200ml. Turn down the heat and slowly whisk in the butter to make a smooth, glossy sauce. Pour into a bowl and set aside to cool completely.

TO ASSEMBLE, spoon some raspberry sauce onto each serving plate and pipe some lines of melted chocolate across the plates. Place a sablé breton base next to the sauce and pipe a generous mound of vanilla cream in the centre.

ARRANGE THE RASPBERRIES around the vanilla cream and dust lightly with icing sugar. Place a scoop of vanilla ice cream next to the raspberry sablé breton. If using, top the vanilla creams with chocolate rectangles and pipe a little blob of vanilla cream on top, then finish with a sugar-coated pistachio. Drizzle each plate with a few drops of reduced stock syrup and scatter a few sugar-coated pistachios around. Serve immediately.

Tiramisu with coffee granita
THIS IS MY TWIST ON A CLASSIC TIRAMISU – A LIGHT COFFEE CREAM SITS ATOP AN ESPRESSO GRANITA AND MASCARPONE SORBET IN A MARTINI GLASS. IN THE RESTAURANT, WE USE A SODA SIPHON TO APPLY THE TIRAMISU CREAM, WHICH CREATES A FROTHY FOAM, BUT THIS SIMPLIFIED VERSION TASTES JUST AS GOOD. *[Illustrated on page 108]*

Serves 6–8

TIRAMISU:
1 sheet of leaf gelatine
2 shots (or 90ml) hot double espresso
50g caster sugar
3 large egg yolks
150g mascarpone
50ml whole milk
75ml double cream

ESPRESSO GRANITA:
150g caster sugar
250ml water
6 shots (or 270ml) single espresso, cooled

MASCARPONE SORBET:
50g caster sugar
100ml water
juice of ½ lemon
25g liquid glucose (or trimoline)
500g mascarpone

TO SERVE:
cocoa powder, to dust
cotton candy (optional)

FIRST, MAKE THE GRANITA. Put the sugar and water into a saucepan and stir over a low heat until the sugar has dissolved. Increase the heat and bring to the boil. Let the syrup boil for 3 minutes then take off the heat. Pour in the espresso and leave to cool completely. Transfer to a shallow, rigid container and freeze for 2–3 hours until partially frozen. Use a fork to break up the semi-frozen granita, stirring the crystallised flakes around the edges into the liquid centre, then return to the freezer. Repeat stirring the mixture 2 or 3 times during freezing until the granita is completely frozen and has a granular texture.

FOR THE MASCARPONE SORBET, put the sugar, water, lemon juice and liquid glucose into a saucepan. Stir over a low heat until the sugar has dissolved, then increase the heat and boil the syrup for a few minutes. Set aside to cool completely.

BEAT THE MASCARPONE in a large bowl to loosen it slightly. Gradually stir in the cooled syrup until evenly incorporated. Transfer to an ice cream machine and churn until almost firm. Scrape the ice cream into a plastic container and freeze until firm.

TO MAKE THE TIRAMISU, soak the gelatine leaf in cold water to cover for a few minutes until soft. Drain and squeeze out excess water, then add to the piping hot espresso and stir until dissolved. Set aside to cool.

MEANWHILE, place the sugar and egg yolks in a large heatproof bowl and beat lightly to mix. Set the bowl over a pan of barely simmering water and whisk the eggs and sugar together, using a hand-held electric beater. Keep beating until the sabayon almost triples in volume and becomes thick and pale. When you lift the beater, the mixture should leave a ribbon trail on the surface that lasts for 10 minutes.

FOLD THE COOLED COFFEE mixture into the sabayon very carefully. Beat the mascarpone, milk and cream together in another bowl, then fold into the coffee sabayon base. Cover the bowl with cling film and chill until ready to serve.

LET THE MASCARPONE SORBET soften at room temperature for about 5 minutes before serving.

TO SERVE, place a heaped tablespoonful of espresso granita in a cocktail glass and add a scoop of mascarpone sorbet. Spoon the tiramisu cream on top and dust with a little cocoa powder. Decorate each serving with a little cotton candy, if you like. Serve at once.

Raspberry, lemon and basil millefeuille with milk ice cream

WAVY CHOCOLATE TUILES ARE LAYERED WITH ALTERNATE BANDS OF RASPBERRY AND LEMON MOUSSE

FOR A STUNNING DESSERT. MAKE THE TUILES AND MILK ICE CREAM WELL IN ADVANCE. YOU CAN ALSO

PREPARE THE STABLE ITALIAN MERINGUE FOR THE MOUSSES A FEW HOURS AHEAD. ASSEMBLE THE

MILLEFEUILLES JUST BEFORE SERVING TO KEEP THE TUILES CRISP. *[Illustrated on page 112]*

Serves 6–8

CHOCOLATE TUILES:
60ml whole milk
75g muscovado sugar
75g icing sugar
150g plain flour
15g cocoa powder
55g egg whites (about 2 large eggs)

ITALIAN MERINGUE:
100g caster sugar
2–3 tbsp water
1 tsp liquid glucose
2 large egg whites

LEMON AND BASIL MOUSSE:
2 sheets of leaf gelatine
50g caster sugar
150ml lemon juice (about 4 lemons)
10 large basil leaves, finely chopped

RASPBERRY MOUSSE:
2 sheets of leaf gelatine
550g raspberries

TO FINISH THE MOUSSES:
400ml double cream

MILK ICE CREAM:
1 litre whole milk
60g condensed milk
5g liquid glucose (or trimoline)

TO SERVE:
melted plain dark chocolate, to drizzle
few tsp crushed nougatine (see page 214), optional
reduced stock syrup (see page 251), optional
handful of raspberries
candied lime zest (optional)

FIRST, MAKE THE MILK ICE CREAM.
Boil the milk in a wide pan until reduced by two-thirds to about 375ml. Mix the condensed milk and liquid glucose in a large bowl. Pour in the reduced milk and stir well. Cool the mixture quickly, by standing the bowl over another bowl of iced water. Then pour into an ice cream machine and churn until almost firm. Turn into a shallow container and freeze.

TO MAKE THE CHOCOLATE TUILES, put the milk and muscovado sugar in a pan and stir over a low heat until the sugar has dissolved. Set aside to cool. Sift the icing sugar, flour and cocoa together into a large bowl. Stir in the cooled milk, a little at a time to avoid lumps forming. Add the egg whites and mix well.

PREHEAT THE OVEN to 180°C/Gas 4. Line a large baking sheet with a silicone liner (silpat or bake-o-glide). Use a palette knife to smooth out a thin layer of the chocolate batter on the liner, then use the edge of the knife to draw 12 x 3cm rectangles. Bake for 6–7 minutes until the chocolate tuiles are fairly firm around the edges. Meanwhile, lay two large thick-handled wooden spoons side-by-side on a board. Leave the tuiles for a few seconds then lift off the liner with a spatula and drape over the spoon handles. The chocolate tuiles will set in a wave fashion and become crisp on cooling. Repeat with the rest of the batter to make at least 24 tuiles. Once cooled, store in an airtight container until ready to serve.

TO MAKE THE ITALIAN MERINGUE, put the sugar, water and liquid glucose in a saucepan and stir over a low heat to dissolve. Once the syrup is clear, increase the heat and boil for 5–7 minutes until it registers 120°C on a sugar thermometer. Meanwhile, whisk the egg whites in a large metal bowl to soft peaks, using an electric beater. Set the bowl on a cloth to stop it moving. Slowly trickle the hot syrup onto the egg white, whisking all the time. Keep whisking for 5 minutes or until the meringue is firm, white and glossy, and the bowl no longer feels hot. Set aside.

TO MAKE THE LEMON MOUSSE, soak the gelatine in cold water to cover for a few minutes to soften. Meanwhile, put the sugar and lemon juice in a small saucepan and stir over a low heat until dissolved. Bring to the boil, then pour into a large bowl. Drain the gelatine, squeeze out excess water and add to the hot lemon syrup, stirring to dissolve. Leave to cool, stirring occasionally.

FOR THE RASPBERRY MOUSSE, soak the gelatine in cold water to soften. Put 400g raspberries in a non-stick pan and stir over a high heat until softened and starting to break up. Tip into a fine sieve set over a large bowl and press to extract all the juice. (If the purée has cooled, reheat to just below the boil.) Drain the gelatine, squeeze out excess liquid and add to the raspberry purée, stirring to dissolve. Cool, stirring occasionally.

DIVIDE THE ITALIAN MERINGUE in half. Fold one portion into the lemon mousse mixture and the other half into the raspberry mixture, in each case until just beginning to set. In another bowl, whip the cream to firm peaks and fold half into each mousse. Fold the chopped basil through the lemon mousse. Finely chop the remaining 150g raspberries and fold through the raspberry mousse. Spoon each mousse into a large piping bag fitted with a large plain nozzle and chill for 2–3 hours.

TO ASSEMBLE THE MILLEFEUILLE, place a chocolate tuile on a clean surface. Pipe a band of lemon mousse along the length of the tuile, then pipe a band of raspberry mousse alongside. Put another chocolate tuile on top. Repeat piping the mousse bands, but this time switching the order so that you end up with alternating colours. Top with a final chocolate tuile. Repeat to assemble a millefeuille for each serving.

TO SERVE, pipe decorative patterns of melted chocolate on each plate if you like. Put two little dollops of mousse on one side of the plate and set a millefeuille on top. Place a neat teaspoon of crushed nougatine on the side if using. Top with a scoop of milk ice cream. Drizzle some melted chocolate over the ice cream and finish each plate with dots of reduced stock syrup if using. Add a little pile of raspberries, topped with candied lime zest if wished. Serve immediately.

Palet d'or with chocolate and hazelnut ice cream and passion fruit cream

THIS IS A RICH, GLOSSY CHOCOLATE GANACHE, MADE ALL THE MORE INTERESTING BY SERVING WITH A CHOCOLATE AND HAZELNUT ICE CREAM, TANGY PASSION FRUIT CREAM AND A SURPRISING GIN JELLY. YOU WILL NEED TO MAKE THE GANACHE AND ASSEMBLE THE DESSERT JUST BEFORE SERVING, BUT ALL THE OTHER COMPONENTS CAN BE MADE IN ADVANCE. *[Illustrated on page 114]*

Serves 6–8

CHOCOLATE GANACHE:
150ml double cream
175g cooking chocolate (about 66% cocoa solids), chopped
30g liquid glucose
30g unsalted butter

CHOCOLATE AND HAZELNUT ICE CREAM:
550ml whole milk
35g liquid glucose
8 large egg yolks
25g caster sugar
200g gianduja paste (chocolate and hazelnut paste) or nutella

GIN GELÉE:
3 sheets of leaf gelatine
250ml gin

SPONGE:
130g unsalted butter, softened to room temperature
110g icing sugar
6 large eggs, separated (yolks lightly beaten)
130g plain dark chocolate, melted and cooled
200g caster sugar
130g plain flour, sifted

CHOCOLATE TUILES:
2 egg whites
90g caster sugar
55g plain flour
1 scant tsp cocoa powder
55g unsalted butter, melted and cooled

PASSION FRUIT CREAM:
125ml double cream
50g caster sugar
juice from 2 passion fruit, strained

TO SERVE (OPTIONAL):
finely crushed cocoa nibs, to sprinkle

FIRST, MAKE THE ICE CREAM. Put the milk and liquid glucose into a saucepan and stir over a low heat until the glucose has melted. Slowly bring to the boil. Meanwhile, beat the egg yolks and sugar in a bowl, then stir in the chocolate and hazelnut paste; the mixture will be quite thick. As soon as the milk starts to boil, take off the heat and slowly pour onto the egg mixture, stirring until smooth.

PASS THROUGH A FINE SIEVE into a clean pan. Stir over a low heat until the custard thickens enough to lightly coat the back of the spoon. Strain through a fine sieve into a bowl. Let cool, stirring every so often to prevent a skin forming. Transfer to an ice cream machine and churn until almost firm. Scoop into a shallow container and freeze until firm.

FOR THE GIN GELÉE, soak the gelatine in cold water to cover for a few minutes to soften. Warm the gin in a small pan but don't let it boil; take off the heat. Drain the gelatine and squeeze out excess water, then add to the gin, stirring until dissolved. Pour into a shallow container and cool completely. Cover and chill for a few hours or overnight to set the jelly.

FOR THE SPONGE, preheat the oven to 160°C/Gas 3. Line a loose-based 30cm square cake tin with baking parchment. Beat the butter and icing sugar together in a large bowl until pale and creamy. Gradually beat in the egg yolks, then fold through the melted chocolate.

WHISK THE EGG WHITES in a clean, dry bowl to firm peaks, using an electric beater. Slowly whisk in the caster sugar, a tablespoonful at a time, to make a firm meringue. Carefully fold the flour into the chocolate batter, then fold in the meringue. Spread the mixture in the tin. Bake for 50 minutes to 1 hour until the sponge feels springy when lightly pressed and a skewer inserted into the centre comes out clean. Leave to cool in the tin.

MEANWHILE, MAKE THE TUILES. Line a baking sheet with silicone liner (silpat or bake-o-glide). Put the egg whites and sugar in a bowl and lightly beat with a fork. Sift in the flour with the cocoa powder and stir to mix well. Add the butter and stir until evenly blended.

USING A PALETTE KNIFE, spread a few thin strips of the tuile mixture on the liner. Bake for 7–8 minutes until brown at the edges, with a matt appearance. Leave to cool for a minute or two. Just before they set, while still pliable, lift each tuile with a palette knife and twist to resemble a pair of wings. Leave to cool and set; they will become crisp and brittle. Repeat making the tuiles until you have used up the batter. Store in an airtight container until ready to serve.

FOR THE PASSION FRUIT CREAM, put the cream and sugar in a small saucepan and stir over a low heat until the sugar has dissolved. Increase the heat and let bubble for 3 minutes.

LOWER THE HEAT, stir in the passion fruit juice and let it simmer for a further 2 minutes or until thickened to a pouring cream consistency. Leave to cool.

AN HOUR BEFORE SERVING, put all the ingredients for the ganache into a double boiler (or heatproof bowl set over a pan of gently simmering water). Stir until the mixture is smooth and shiny. Keep warm while assembling the dessert.

TRIM THE SIDES and top of the sponge to even out, then cut into 12 or 16 neat squares. Spread a layer of ganache over one square then sandwich with another, with the flat side facing upwards. Repeat with the remaining sponge squares. Place the sponge sandwiches on a wire rack set over a baking tray.

POUR A LAYER OF GANACHE over each sponge sandwich to cover, allowing the excess to drip down the sides. Use a palette knife to smooth the ganache around the sides. Leave for 30–40 minutes to allow the ganache to firm up.

TO PLATE, spoon the passion fruit cream decoratively onto the serving plates. Using a clean palette knife, carefully lift a ganache-covered sponge onto each plate. Put a spoonful of gin gelée alongside. If using, sprinkle a little crushed cocoa nib on the plates. Top each palet d'or with a chocolate tuile and a neat scoop of chocolate and hazelnut ice cream. Serve immediately.

Slow-baked quince with crème catalan, Pedro Ximenez gelée and acacia honey granita

THIS SPANISH-INSPIRED DESSERT COMBINES SOME OF MY FAVOURITE FLAVOURS – AROMATIC SHERRY, SWEET QUINCE AND CREAMY CUSTARD. PREPARE ALL THE ELEMENTS FOR THIS DESSERT WELL AHEAD, READY TO ASSEMBLE JUST BEFORE SERVING. SPREAD ANY LEFTOVER QUINCE PURÉE ON WALNUT BREAD AND SERVE WITH MEMBRILLO CHEESE. *[Illustrated on page 115]*

Serves about 8

QUINCE PURÉE:
2 large quinces, cleaned
225g caster sugar
2 vanilla pods, split

ACACIA HONEY GRANITA:
175g acacia honey
625ml water
1½ sheets of leaf gelatine

PEDRO XIMENEZ JELLY:
375ml Pedro Ximenez sherry
3 sheets of leaf gelatine

CRÈME CATALAN:
500ml whipping cream
80ml whole milk
½ vanilla pod, split
60g caster sugar
2 large egg yolks

MINT CUSTARD:
250ml whole milk
250ml double cream
small bunch of mint (about 6 sprigs), leaves only
60g caster sugar
6 large egg yolks

TO SERVE:
8–10 good-quality madeleines (optional)
16–20 thin tuiles sandwiched with quince purée (optional)

FIRST, MAKE THE QUINCE PURÉE. Preheat the oven to 140°C/Gas 1. Peel the quinces, then cut into quarters and remove the core. Roughly chop the flesh into small cubes and place in a wide ovenproof pan with the sugar. Pour in enough water to cover and stir over a low heat until the sugar has dissolved. Scrape out the vanilla seeds and add to the pan with the empty pods. Increase the heat and bring the syrup to the boil. Turn off the heat, cover the pan with a piece of foil and place in the oven.

BAKE FOR ABOUT 3 HOURS until the quince is very soft. While still hot, drain the quince, reserving the liquor and put into a food processor or blender with a little of the cooking syrup. Whiz to a smooth purée. If too thick, blend in a little more of the reserved syrup. Cool completely, then chill until ready to use.

NEXT, MAKE THE GRANITA. Put the honey and water in a saucepan and bring to the boil, stirring once or twice. Soak the gelatine leaves in cold water for a few minutes to soften. Boil the honey syrup until it begins to foam, then strain through a fine sieve into a wide bowl. Drain the gelatine leaves, squeeze out excess water and add to the hot syrup, stirring until the gelatine dissolves. Leave to cool completely, stirring every once in a while, then pour the mixture into a shallow container, cover and freeze for 2 hours until partially frozen.

USE A FORK TO STIR the ice crystals into the still liquid centre. Freeze for another 1–2 hours, then beat the mixture again and return to the freezer. Beat the mixture twice more during freezing to achieve a granular texture.

FOR THE JELLY, pour the sherry into a small pan and place over a low heat. Meanwhile, soak the gelatine leaves in cold water for a few minutes to soften. When the sherry is hot enough for you to feel the heat rising from the pan (but not boiling), take off the heat. Take the gelatine leaves and squeeze out excess water, then add to the sherry and gently swirl the pan until the gelatine has dissolved. Leave to cool completely.

SPOON A THIN LAYER of quince purée into individual serving glasses. Carefully pour a layer of sherry jelly over the purée, using a teaspoon to guide the liquid in if you find it easier. Chill for a few hours or overnight until the jelly is softly set.

TO MAKE THE CRÈME CATALAN, pour the cream and milk into a heavy-based saucepan. Scrape the vanilla seeds into the pan and add the pod too. Slowly bring to the boil. Meanwhile, beat the sugar and egg yolks together in a large bowl. When the creamy milk begins to bubble up the side of the pan, take off the heat. Slowly pour onto the sugar and yolks, whisking continuously as you do so. Strain the mixture through a fine sieve into a clean pan.

STIR CONSTANTLY with a wooden spoon over a low heat until the mixture thickens into a light custard. It should coat the back of the spoon and leave an impression when you draw a finger down the spoon. Remove from the heat and strain through a fine sieve into a wide bowl. Leave to cool, stirring the custard occasionally to prevent a skin forming. Cover and chill until required.

FOR THE MINT CUSTARD, bring the milk and cream to the boil in a heavy-based saucepan, then immediately remove from the heat and add the mint leaves. Leave to cool and infuse for 30 minutes. Beat the sugar and egg yolks together in a bowl. Strain the mint-infused cream onto the mixture, then return to the clean pan. Stir over a low heat until it thickens into a light custard (as for the crème catalan, left and above). Again, strain the custard through a fine sieve into a wide bowl and leave to cool completely, stirring occasionally to prevent a skin forming. Pour the custard into a jug.

TO ASSEMBLE, whisk the crème catalan to lighten it. Spoon a layer over the sherry jelly in each glass. Stand the glasses on serving plates. Top with a neat quenelle of acacia honey granita. If you like, serve a Madeleine and a quince tuile on the side. Bring the desserts to the table and drizzle a little mint custard on top of the crème catalan as you serve.

Chocolate parfait with passion fruit and guava coulis IN THE

RESTAURANT WE USE GIANDUJA PASTE TO MAKE THESE PARFAITS. IT LENDS A LOVELY RICH FLAVOUR

BUT IS ONLY AVAILABLE COMMERCIALLY, SO HERE I HAVE USED DARK CHOCOLATE INSTEAD. SIMILARLY

WE OBTAIN OUR GUAVA AND PASSION FRUIT PURÉES COMMERCIALLY. THIS COULIS LENDS AN EQUALLY

GOOD FLAVOUR, BUT IT WILL NOT HAVE QUITE THE SAME INTENSITY OF COLOUR. *[Illustrated on page 118]*

Serves 10–12

CHOCOLATE PARFAIT:
8 large egg yolks
150g caster sugar
100ml water
360ml double cream
40ml whole milk
150g plain dark chocolate, melted and cooled
100ml vodka

PASSION FRUIT AND GUAVA COULIS:
500ml guava juice
juice from 8 ripe passion fruit, strained
40ml stock syrup (see page 251)
2 tsp arrowroot
1 tsp water

TO SERVE:
melted plain dark chocolate, to pipe
cocoa powder, to dust (optional)

FOR THE PARFAIT, prepare a pate à bombe with the egg yolks and sugar: dissolve the sugar in the water in a heavy-based saucepan over a low heat, then increase the heat to high and bring the syrup to the boil. Meanwhile, whisk the egg yolks in a large bowl, using an electric beater, until pale and creamy. Boil the syrup until it registers 120°C on a sugar thermometer. With the machine on the highest speed, slowly trickle the hot syrup onto the egg yolks. Keep on whisking until the mixture is thick and smooth and has substantially increased in volume. Whisk until the bowl no longer feels hot, then set aside to cool.

IN ANOTHER BOWL, whisk the cream and milk with an electric beater to soft peaks. Fold the melted chocolate into the pate à bombe, then fold in the whipped cream and finally the vodka. Spoon the parfait into 150ml individual moulds (such as darioles or other shaped moulds) and cover with cling film. Freeze for a few hours or overnight until firm.

FOR THE COULIS, boil the guava juice until reduced to 200ml. Add the passion fruit juice and stock syrup. Mix the arrowroot with the 1 tsp water, then add to the pan. Stir over a low-to-medium heat until the mixture is smooth and has thickened to a shiny, syrupy sauce. Pass through a fine sieve into a bowl and leave to cool completely. Transfer the coulis to a plastic squeezy bottle and chill until ready to use.

TO SERVE, pipe lines of melted chocolate on each chilled serving plate to create a decorative square (as shown). Fill the squares with the passion fruit and guava coulis, using the back of a teaspoon to help spread the sauce if necessary. Set aside.

UNMOULD THE PARFAITS one at a time. Dip the base of the mould into a bowl of hot water for a few seconds, then run a thin knife along the edges of the parfait to loosen it. Tip onto a board or large plate and dust with cocoa powder if using. (At the restaurant, we use a special spray gun to dust the parfaits with cocoa powder. You may not be able to achieve such an even result without one, but that won't affect the taste.) Use a palette knife to transfer the parfait to a decorated plate. Keep chilled while you assemble the rest of the plates. Serve at once.

Bitter chocolate mousse with coffee granita and light ginger

cream THIS GORGEOUS DESSERT IS SO POPULAR WITH OUR CUSTOMERS, IT IS FAST BECOMING A

CLASSIC. WE OFTEN VARY THE TYPE OF MOUSSE IN THE CHOCOLATE CYLINDER – ALTERNATING

BETWEEN GIANDUJA, PRALINE AND DARK CHOCOLATE. YOU WILL NEED TO PREPARE THE DIFFERENT

ELEMENTS OF THIS DESSERT IN ADVANCE, READY TO ASSEMBLE JUST BEFORE SERVING. *[Illustrated on page 119]*

Serves 6

CHOCOLATE CYLINDER:
300g dark couverture chocolate (see page 252), chopped

BITTER CHOCOLATE MOUSSE:
110g plain dark chocolate (minimum 75% cocoa solids), broken into small pieces
40g butter
3 egg yolks
100g caster sugar
75ml water
100ml double cream
90g (about 2 large) egg whites

CARAMELISED RICE CRISPIES:
50g caster sugar
40g rice crispies

LIGHT GINGER FOAM:
75g double cream
175ml whole milk
35g caster sugar
15g fresh ginger, peeled and grated
¾ sheet of leaf gelatine

TO SERVE:
melted plain dark chocolate, to decorate
6 brownie squares (see page 241)
6 small tbsp espresso granita (see page 228)
6 pieces of chocolate sticks (optional)
6 small pieces of edible gold leaf (optional)
6 scoops of milk ice cream (see page 230)

FOR THE CHOCOLATE CYLINDERS, you first need to temper the chocolate. For this, you will need a digital probe thermometer to assess the temperature of the chocolate. Set aside 55g of the chopped couverture. Place the rest in a glass mixing bowl and microwave on high for 30 seconds at a time until most of the chocolate has melted. Give it a stir each time and gauge the temperature – you want it to reach 45°C, no more than a degree or two higher.

ADD THE REMAINING CHOCOLATE and stir constantly. Let the temperature of the combined chocolate fall to 27°C, then microwave in 5–10 second bursts until the temperature climbs up to 31°C. To test if it is tempered, dip the tip of a palette knife into the chocolate, tap off any excess and leave to set for 5 minutes. It should harden in a few minutes and have a shiny gloss. If not, repeat the tempering process. (Note: do not overheat the chocolate as it cannot be tempered again once it has seized.)

ONCE TEMPERED, stand the bowl of chocolate in a larger bowl of lukewarm water to maintain the temperature at about 31°C.

TO MAKE THE CYLINDERS, you will need seven 6cm round metal cutters, a large sheet of acetate and 6 acetate rectangles, each about 8 x 20cm. Using a small palette knife, spread a 2mm layer of tempered chocolate over each acetate rectangle and let it set a little. When the chocolate begins to firm up, carefully curve the acetate into a metal cutter so that it forms a cylinder. If you wish, tape the overlapping ends of the acetate to secure the shape of the cylinder. Using the back of a teaspoon, smooth a little more chocolate over the area where the ends of the acetate meet, to seal the cylinder. Repeat to make 6 cylinders (or more to to allow for possible breakages during the final assembly).

TO MAKE THE ROUND TOPS, spread the tempered chocolate on the large piece of acetate and then leave to set a little. As the chocolate begins to firm up, use the remaining metal cutter to press down and outline 6 circles. (You might like to use any remaining tempered chocolate to make extra tops, to allow for possible breakages.) Let the chocolate cylinders and tops set in a cool part of the kitchen.

TO MAKE THE CARAMELISED RICE CRISPIES, line a tray with silicone liner (silpat or bake-o-glide) or lightly oil a baking tray and set aside. Scatter the sugar evenly in a dry, heavy-based pan and place over a high heat. Let the sugar dissolve and cook to a golden caramel. Remove the pan from the heat, add the rice crispies and toss to coat, then immediately tip onto the oiled tray. Tilt the tray to spread out the mixture and set aside to cool; the caramel will firm up and become brittle when cooled. Break the caramelised rice crispies into smaller pieces, then chop finely. Store in an airtight container until ready to use.

FOR THE GINGER FOAM, put the cream, milk and sugar into a saucepan and bring to the boil. Turn off the heat, add the grated ginger and leave to infuse for 5 minutes. Meanwhile, soak the gelatine in cold water to cover for a few minutes to soften. Strain the infused cream through a fine sieve into a bowl and discard the ginger. Drain the gelatine, squeeze out excess water, then add to the warm cream and stir until it has dissolved. Chill the mixture for a few hours until it has partially set.

WHISK THE GINGER MIXTURE, using an electric beater, for 5 minutes until it is light and foamy. Return to the fridge and chill for another hour or two until set.

[continued overleaf]

FOR THE CHOCOLATE MOUSSE, melt the chocolate and butter together in a heatproof bowl set over a pan of barely simmering water. Cool slightly, stirring the mixture every once in a while.

NEXT, MAKE A PATE À BOMBE with the egg yolks and sugar: dissolve the sugar in the water in a heavy-based saucepan over a low heat, then increase the heat to high and bring the syrup to the boil. Meanwhile, whisk the egg yolks in a large bowl, using an electric beater, until pale and creamy. Boil the syrup until it registers 120°C on a sugar thermometer. With the machine on the highest speed, slowly trickle the hot syrup onto the egg yolks. Keep on whisking until the mixture is thick and smooth and has substantially increased in volume. Whisk until the bowl no longer feels hot, then set aside to cool to room temperature.

WHIP THE CREAM TO SOFT PEAKS. In another clean, dry bowl, whisk the egg whites to soft peaks. Fold the chocolate mixture into the pate à bombe, then fold in the whipped cream and finally the whisked egg whites.

JUST BEFORE SERVING, whisk up the ginger foam again until it is thick and creamy, then transfer to a piping bag fitted with a large plain nozzle.

TO ASSEMBLE, pipe decorative chocolate lines on 6 serving plates. Cut the brownie squares horizontally to get 3–4mm thick slices. Using a round metal cutter slightly smaller than the chocolate cylinders, cut out discs from each brownie slice. Place a brownie disc on a serving plate. Carefully position a chocolate cylinder over the brownie disc. Cut off any tape with a knife and slowly and carefully unravel the acetate, pulling it away from the chocolate cylinder.

PIPE IN THE BITTER CHOCOLATE mousse to half-fill the cylinder. Sprinkle a little caramelised rice crispie on top, then add a tablespoonful of espresso granita. Pipe the ginger cream on top to come up slightly above the edge of the cylinder. Carefully remove a round chocolate disc from the acetate. If using, attach a chocolate stick and a small piece of gold leaf to the disc, using a bit of melted chocolate as glue. Set on top of the ginger foam. Place a scoop of milk ice cream on a little bed of rice crispie praline on the side of the plate and drizzle over a little melted chocolate if you like. Serve at once.

Apple parfait with honeycomb, bitter chocolate and champagne foam

THIS IS AN IMPRESSIVE DESSERT, THOUGH RATHER TIME-CONSUMING TO PREPARE AT HOME. YOU COULD SIMPLIFY THE RECIPE BY OMITTING THE HONEYCOMB TUILES, MILK ICE CREAM AND CHOCOLATE SPIRALS. YOU WILL HAVE EXTRA BROWNIES TO SERVE ON THE SIDE, OR THE FOLLOWING DAY. *[Illustrated on page 109]*

Serves 8

APPLE PARFAIT:

4 large egg yolks (80g in total)
110g caster sugar
75ml water
3 Granny Smith apples
squeeze of lemon juice
400ml pure apple juice
3½ sheets of leaf gelatine
150ml double cream
100ml apple Bacardi (or clear rum)

BROWNIE:

140g plain flour
60g cocoa powder
140g unsalted butter, softened to
  room temperature
340g caster sugar
4 large eggs, lightly beaten
130g plain dark chocolate, chopped

APPLE GRANITA:

4 Granny Smith apples
juice of 1 lemon
200g caster sugar
400ml water
4 tbsp liquid glucose

HONEYCOMB TUILES:

165g caster sugar
60g liquid glucose
70g runny honey
40ml water
20g bicarbonate of soda

CHAMPAGNE FOAM:

50g caster sugar
50ml whole milk
1 sheet of leaf gelatine
250ml Champagne
100ml double cream

TO SERVE:

melted plain dark chocolate, to decorate
lightly toasted desiccated coconut, to
  sprinkle (optional)
1 tsp crushed honeycomb (see recipe)
8 scoops of milk ice cream (see page 230)
chocolate spirals, to decorate (optional)
reduced apple syrup, to drizzle (optional)

[continued overleaf]

FIRST, MAKE THE BROWNIE. Preheat the oven to 160°C/Gas 3. Line a 20cm square baking tin with baking parchment. Sift together the flour and cocoa powder. Put the butter and sugar in a large bowl and beat with an electric beater until pale and fluffy. Gradually mix in the beaten eggs, a little at a time. Carefully fold in the sifted flour mixture followed by the chopped chocolate. Spread the mixture in the prepared baking tin and bake for 25–35 minutes until the brownie has set around the edges and feels fairly firm in the centre. Unlike a conventional brownie it should be more set in the middle so that it can be sliced horizontally into thin squares or rectangles.

LEAVE THE BROWNIE TO COOL in the tin for 10 minutes, then transfer to a wire rack and leave to cool completely.

NEXT, MAKE THE APPLE GRANITA. Leaving the skins on, quarter and core the apples and immediately toss with the lemon juice. Place the apples in a single layer in plastic containers and freeze for an hour to chill thoroughly and help intensify the colour.

MEANWHILE, dissolve the sugar in the water in a heavy-based pan over a low heat. When the syrup is clear, increase the heat and boil for about 5 minutes until slightly reduced. Cool completely, then stir in the liquid glucose.

REMOVE THE APPLES from the freezer and chop them roughly. Put them in a food processor with a third of the sugar syrup and whiz until finely puréed, stopping to scrape down the sides of the processor once or twice. Mix with the rest of the syrup, then pass the mixture through a fine sieve into a large bowl. Rub the pulp in the sieve with the back of a ladle to extract all the juice.

POUR THE APPLE PURÉE into a shallow plastic container and freeze for 2–3 hours until it is partially frozen. Remove and stir the frozen crystals into the liquid using a fork, then return to the freezer. Repeat stirring the granita twice more during freezing to obtain a granular texture.

NOW PREPARE THE BROWNIE BASE for the parfait. Line eight 4 x 8cm rectangular moulds with cling film, then cut out a thin slice of brownie to line the base of each one. To do this, cut the brownie into 4 x 8cm rectangles. Turn one on its side and cut into 3 or 4 thin slices; repeat to obtain 8 thin slices (you will have some brownies leftover for tea the next day!). Press a brownie slice into each lined mould. If you do not have suitable rectangular moulds, line a 1 litre loaf tin with cling film, then cut thin slices of chocolate brownie to fit the base of the tin.

TO MAKE THE APPLE PARFAIT, prepare a pate à bombe with the egg yolks and sugar: dissolve the sugar in the water in a heavy-based saucepan over a low heat, then increase the heat to high and bring the syrup to the boil. Meanwhile, whisk the egg yolks in a large bowl, using an electric beater, until pale and creamy. Boil the syrup until it registers 120°C on a sugar thermometer. With the machine on the highest speed, slowly trickle the hot syrup onto the egg yolks. Keep on whisking until the mixture is thick and smooth and has substantially increased in volume. Whisk until the bowl no longer feels hot, then set aside to cool to room temperature.

PEEL, CORE AND CHOP the apples, squeezing over a little lemon juice to prevent them discolouring. Put them in a food processor with the apple juice and blend to a fine, smooth purée. Transfer to a pan and bring to the boil. Cook until the purée has reduced by about half, to 450g. Meanwhile, soak the gelatine in cold water for a few minutes to soften.

PASS THE REDUCED APPLE PURÉE through a fine sieve into a large bowl, pushing down on the pulp in the sieve to extract all the juice. (If the purée has cooled down, reheat to just below the boil in a pan, then tip into a bowl.) Drain the gelatine and squeeze out excess water, then add to the hot apple purée, stirring to dissolve. Allow to cool, stirring the mixture every once in as it cools.

WHEN THE PATE À BOMBE and apple purée have both cooled down to room temperature, fold the purée into the pate à bombe. Whip the cream to soft peaks, then gradually incorporate the rum a little at a time. Fold this into the parfait base mixture, then spoon into the prepared moulds or loaf tin and freeze until firm.

TO MAKE THE HONEYCOMB TUILES, preheat the oven to 190°C/Gas 5. Put the sugar, glucose, honey and water into a heavy-based saucepan and stir over a low heat until the sugar has dissolved. Increase the heat and boil until the syrup registers 170°C on a sugar thermometer and begins to take on a caramel colour. Whisk in the bicarbonate of soda until smooth; take care as the mixture will erupt and dramatically increase in volume. Tip onto a baking sheet lined with a silicone liner (silpat or bake-o-glide) or a lightly oiled baking tray. Leave to cool completely until the honeycomb is hard and brittle.

BREAK THE HONEYCOMB into smaller pieces. Lightly crush one or two pieces and reserve for decoration. Put the rest of the honeycomb in a food processor and whiz to a fine powder.

CUT A RECTANGULAR TEMPLATE (4 x 8cm) and set on a large baking tray lined with a silicone liner. (We use templates cut out from the lids of plastic containers at the restaurant.) Sift enough honeycomb powder over the cut-out to get a thin layer. Lift off the template and repeat to make 16 rectangles or more to allow for breakage (you may need to use two baking sheets). Bake in the oven for 1 minute or until the honeycomb powder has just melted. Leave to cool completely, then lift the rectangles off the silicone liner and store in an airtight container until ready to use.

FOR THE CHAMPAGNE FOAM, put the sugar and milk in a pan over a low heat and stir to dissolve, then slowly bring to the boil. Meanwhile, soak the gelatine leaf in cold water to cover for a few minutes to soften. Remove the gelatine and squeeze out excess water. As the milk begins to boil, take off the heat and add the gelatine, stirring to dissolve. Leave to cool completely.

STIR THE CHAMPAGNE into the milk mixture just as it begins to set, then chill for 2–3 hours until firm but still slightly wobbly to the touch in the centre. Whisk the mixture using an electric beater to lighten it. In another bowl, whip the cream until it holds peaks, then fold into the Champagne base. Whisk the mixture until it is light, then chill for a couple of hours before serving.

WHEN READY TO SERVE, brush each serving plate with a strip of melted chocolate and sprinkle with desiccated coconut if you like. Unmould the apple parfaits by rubbing a hot cloth around the sides of the rectangular moulds (or loaf tin). Turn out and remove the cling film. Use a palette knife to lift each parfait onto a serving plate. (If you have used a loaf tin, trim the edges of the parfait to get straight sides, then cut into thick slices.)

DRIZZLE MELTED CHOCOLATE decoratively over the top of the parfait, then top with a layer of apple granita. Sandwich the parfait vertically with two honeycomb tuiles. Put a neat spoonful of Champagne foam on one side of the parfait and sprinkle a little crushed honeycomb on top. Add a scoop of milk ice cream and decorate with a chocolate spiral if you like. Drizzle the plate with a little reduced apple syrup if using. Serve immediately.

BASICS

Fish stock

MAKES ABOUT 1 LITRE

1kg white fish bones and trimmings (ideally turbot, sole or haddock)
2 tbsp olive oil
1 small onion, peeled and chopped
½ celery stalk, trimmed and sliced
1 small fennel bulb, trimmed and chopped
1 small leek, trimmed and sliced
sea salt and black pepper
75ml dry white wine

If using the fish heads, cut out the eyes and gills and remove any traces of blood. Heat the olive oil in a stockpot or large pan and add the onion, celery, fennel, leek and a little salt and pepper. Stir over a medium heat for 3–4 minutes until the vegetables begin to soften; don't let them brown. Add the fish bones and wine and let bubble until reduced right down. Pour in enough cold water to cover and bring to the boil, then skim off the scum from the surface. Lower the heat and simmer for 20 minutes. Remove the pan from the heat and allow the stock to settle for about 20 minutes as it cools. Ladle the stock through a muslin-lined sieve into a bowl. Chill and use within 2–3 days, or freeze in smaller quantities for up to 3 months.

Shellfish stock

MAKES ABOUT 1 LITRE

4 tbsp olive oil
500g lobster, langoustine or crab shells and heads (or a mixture)
bones from 2–3 red mullet
50g shallots, peeled and roughly chopped
1 celery stalk, trimmed and chopped
1 carrot, peeled and chopped
¼ leek, halved
2 garlic cloves, peeled
50g red pepper trimmings
50g fennel trimmings
25g tomato purée
few thyme sprigs
few parsley stalks
1 bay leaf
3 coriander seeds
3 white peppercorns
1 star anise
125ml dry white wine or Noilly Prat
1 litre fish stock (see left)
sea salt and black pepper

Heat half the olive oil in a large pan. Add the shells and fish bones and fry, shaking the pan and stirring occasionally, until the shells are bright red. Meanwhile, heat the remaining oil in a wide stockpot and add the shallots, celery, carrot, leek, garlic and red pepper and fennel trimmings. Cook, stirring occasionally, for about 8–10 minutes until softened. Stir in the tomato purée and cook for a further 2 minutes. Tip in the herbs and spices and add the wine. Let bubble until almost totally reduced, then add the fish stock. Bring to a simmer, skim off any scum from the surface and cook gently for 30 minutes. Season lightly. Remove from the heat and allow the stock to settle for about 20 minutes as it cools. Pass the stock through a muslin-lined sieve. Use as required within 2–3 days, or freeze in batches for up to 3 months.

Chicken stock

MAKES ABOUT 1.5 LITRES

2 tbsp olive oil
1 carrot, peeled and chopped
1 onion, peeled and chopped
2 celery stalks, trimmed and chopped
1 leek, trimmed and sliced
3 garlic cloves, peeled
2 bay leaves
few thyme sprigs
2 tbsp tomato purée
2 tbsp plain flour
1kg raw chicken bones (roasted if making brown chicken stock)
sea salt and black pepper

Heat the olive oil in a large stockpot. Add the vegetables, garlic, bay leaves and thyme and cook over a medium heat, stirring occasionally, until the vegetables are golden. Stir in the tomato purée and flour and cook for another minute. Add the chicken bones and pour in enough cold water to cover them. Season lightly. Bring to the boil and skim off any scum and froth that rises to the surface. Reduce the heat to a simmer and leave to cook gently for an hour. Let the stock settle and cool down for 20 minutes before passing it through a fine sieve. Chill and use within 4–5 days, or freeze in batches for up to 3 months.

Veal stock

MAKES ABOUT 1.5–2 LITRES

1.5kg veal bones
100ml olive oil
1 large onion, peeled and roughly chopped
2 large carrots, peeled and chopped
1 celery stalk, trimmed and chopped
4–5 garlic cloves (unpeeled)
1 tbsp tomato purée
175ml Madeira
175ml ruby port
100g chestnut mushrooms, cleaned
bouquet garni (bay leaf, thyme and flat leaf parsley sprigs)
sea salt and black pepper

Preheat the oven to 220°C/Gas 7. Put the veal bones into a roasting pan, drizzle over half of the olive oil and roast for 1–1½ hours, turning occasionally, until browned. Meanwhile, heat the remaining olive oil in a large stockpot and fry the chopped vegetables and garlic cloves over a high heat until lightly coloured. Stir in the tomato purée and fry for another 2 minutes until the vegetables are golden brown. Deglaze the pan with the Madeira and port and boil vigorously until reduced to a syrupy consistency. Drain the roasted bones of excess oil and add to the stockpot. Pour in enough water to cover, about 5 litres, and bring to the boil. Skim off the scum that rises to the surface, then reduce the heat to a gentle simmer and add the mushrooms and bouquet garni. Simmer gently for about 6 hours, skimming every once in a while, until the stock is clear. Leave the stock to settle and cool a little, then strain through a muslin-lined colander set over a large bowl. For a more intense flavour, pour the stock into a clean pan and boil until reduced by half. Season lightly. Chill and use within 4–5 days, or freeze in batches for up to 3 months.

Vegetable stock

MAKES ABOUT 1.5 LITRES

3 onions, peeled and roughly chopped
1 leek, trimmed and chopped
2 celery stalks, trimmed and chopped
6 carrots, peeled and chopped
½ head of garlic, split horizontally
1 bay leaf
½ tsp white peppercorns
½ tsp black peppercorns
handful of herb sprigs (such as thyme, basil, tarragon, coriander and parsley)
200ml dry white wine
sea salt and black pepper

Put all the vegetables in a large stockpot with the garlic, bay leaf and peppercorns. Pour in enough cold water to cover, about 2 litres, and bring to the boil. Lower the heat and simmer gently for 20 minutes. Remove the pan from the heat, then add the herb sprigs, wine and a little seasoning. Give the stock a stir and leave to cool completely. If you have time, chill the stock overnight before straining. Otherwise, pass through a fine sieve once cooled. Use within 5 days or freeze in batches for up to 3 months.

Lamb jus

MAKES ABOUT 1.2 LITRES

1kg lamb rib or neck bones
60ml olive oil
1 onion, peeled and chopped
2 carrots, peeled and chopped
1 celery stalk, trimmed and chopped
½ head of garlic, split horizontally
1½ tsp tomato purée
1 bay leaf
few thyme sprigs
few flat leaf parsley sprigs
500ml dry white wine
1 litre veal stock (see left)
1 litre chicken stock (see left)

Preheat the oven to 200°C/Gas 6. Put the lamb bones in a large roasting pan and drizzle with half the olive oil. Roast for about an hour, turning occasionally, until well browned. Heat the remaining oil in a stockpot, add the vegetables and brown over a high heat, stirring frequently. Add the tomato purée and herbs and stir for another minute or two. Deglaze the pan with the wine, then boil until reduced by half. Drain the browned lamb bones of excess oil, then add to the stockpot. Pour in the veal and chicken stocks and top up with a little water if necessary, to ensure the bones are covered. Bring to the boil and skim off the scum from the surface. Reduce the heat to a simmer and cook for 4 hours, until the liquid has reduced by about half. Leave to settle and cool slightly, then strain the stock through a muslin-lined sieve. Use within 5 days or freeze in batches for up to 3 months.

Red wine sauce

MAKES ABOUT 450ML
2 tbsp olive oil
*3 banana shallots, peeled and finely
  chopped*
*about 100g (or more) meat trimmings
  (beef, veal, venison or poultry)*
1/2 tsp black peppercorns
few thyme sprigs
1 bay leaf
1 tbsp sherry vinegar (or red wine vinegar)
750ml red wine
400ml chicken stock (see page 246)
400ml veal stock (see page 247)
sea salt and black pepper

Heat the olive oil in a wide heavy-based
saucepan and sauté the shallots for 4–6
minutes until they are soft and begin to
caramelise. Add the meat trimmings and
fry for a few minutes until browned. Add
the peppercorns, thyme, bay leaf and
sherry vinegar. Deglaze the pan with the
red wine and bring to the boil. Boil the
liquor rapidly until reduced by three-
quarters to a rich syrupy glaze. Add the
chicken and veal stocks and return to the
boil. Once again, boil vigorously until the
sauce has reduced by half, or until it has
reached the desired consistency. Strain
through a fine sieve into a bowl and
adjust the seasoning. Reheat to serve.

Madeira sauce

MAKES ABOUT 500ML
2 tbsp olive oil
2 banana shallots, peeled and chopped
1 bay leaf
few thyme sprigs
1 garlic clove, peeled
*about 100g (or more) meat trimmings
  (pork, beef or poultry)*
250ml Madeira
150ml port
500ml veal stock (see page 247)
500ml chicken stock (see page 246)
sea salt and black pepper

Heat the olive oil in a wide saucepan, add
the shallots with the herbs and garlic and
sweat for 4–6 minutes until softened. Add
the meat trimmings and fry for a few
minutes until browned. Deglaze the pan
with the Madeira and port and let bubble
until reduced by two-thirds. Pour in the
veal and chicken stocks and bring back to
the boil. Reduce again by two-thirds or
until the sauce has thickened to a syrupy
consistency. Pass through a fine sieve into
a bowl. Taste and adjust the seasoning.

Truffle-infused Madeira sauce: Add 1–2
tbsp truffle trimmings with the stocks.

Herb crisps

drizzle of olive oil
*herb leaves, such as basil, flat leaf parsley,
  coriander or mint*

Stretch a sheet of cling film tightly over a
deep plate. Rub a little olive oil over the
herb leaves and press them flat on to the
cling film. Microwave for 2½–3 minutes
or until crisp. Store in an airtight
container and use within a day or two.

Lemongrass and chervil velouté

MAKES ABOUT 500ML
1 shallot, peeled and sliced
1/2 tsp white peppercorns
1/2 tsp coriander seeds
1 garlic clove
1 bay leaf
few thyme sprigs
2 lemongrass stalks, split
125ml Noilly Prat (or other dry vermouth)
250ml fish stock (see page 246)
250ml double cream
sea salt and black pepper
bunch of chervil, leaves only, chopped

Put the shallot, peppercorns, coriander
seeds, garlic, bay leaf, thyme, lemongrass
and vermouth in a wide saucepan and
bring to the boil. Let bubble until the
liquid has reduced down to a syrupy
glaze. Add the stock and boil to reduce by
half. Add the cream and simmer until the
sauce has reduced to a coating
consistency. Taste and adjust the
seasoning. Strain the sauce through a fine
sieve into a bowl. Just before serving,
reheat and stir in the chopped chervil.

Tomato concassé

MAKES ABOUT 150G
250g ripe plum tomatoes

Lightly score a cross on the top and base
of each tomato. Put them in a heatproof
bowl and pour on boiling water to cover.
Leave for 45 seconds to 1 minute until
the skins can be peeled off easily; no
longer or the tomatoes will turn soft.
Remove and peel away the skins, then
quarter and remove the seeds. Chop into
a fine dice. Cover and chill until required.

Tomato sauce

MAKES ABOUT 175ML
200g ripe plum tomatoes
75ml olive oil
1 banana shallot, peeled and diced
1 garlic clove, peeled and crushed
sea salt and black pepper

Immerse the plum tomatoes in a bowl of boiling water for 45 seconds to 1 minute. Remove and peel away the skins, then quarter, deseed and chop the flesh. Heat the olive oil in a pan and gently sweat the shallot and garlic for 4–6 minutes until softened but not browned. Add the chopped tomatoes and season well. Increase the heat and cook for 8–10 minutes until the tomatoes are very soft. Whiz in a blender until smooth, then return the sauce to the pan and heat through. Taste and adjust the seasoning.

Mayonnaise

MAKES ABOUT 600ML
4 large egg yolks
2 tsp white wine vinegar
2 tsp English mustard
1 tsp fine sea salt
freshly grated black pepper
600ml groundnut oil (or light olive oil)
1–2 tbsp cold water

Put the egg yolks, wine vinegar, mustard, salt and some pepper into a food processor and whiz until the mixture is very thick and creamy. With the motor running, slowly trickle in the oil in a fine, steady stream. Blend in the water as well; this will help to stabilise the emulsion. Taste and adjust the seasoning. Transfer the mayonnaise to a bowl or jar, cover and refrigerate. Use within 3 days.

Classic vinaigrette

MAKES ABOUT 250ML
100ml extra virgin olive oil
100ml groundnut oil
3 tbsp white wine vinegar
1 scant tsp Dijon mustard
sea salt and black pepper

Whiz all the ingredients together in a bowl using a hand-held stick blender until emulsified. Pour into a squeezy bottle (or a screw-topped jar) and keep in the fridge. Shake well before each use.

Port vinaigrette: Boil 600ml port in a wide pan to reduce by half until thick and syrupy. Cool slightly, then whiz in a blender with 100ml classic vinaigrette to emulsify. Pour into a clean squeezy bottle ready for drizzling. Refrigerate and shake well before each use. Makes about 400ml.

Basil vinaigrette

MAKES ABOUT 70ML
1 large bunch of basil, about 80g
60ml olive oil
pinch of fine sea salt
2–3 tsp lemon juice, to taste

Strip the basil leaves from their stalks, add to a pot of boiling water and blanch for 40 seconds, then drain and refresh in a bowl of iced water. Drain well and gently squeeze out excess water. Put the leaves into a small food processor with the olive oil and salt and blend to a fine purée. Press through a sieve into a bowl and discard the pulp. If not using immediately, keep in a squeezy bottle (or a clean jar) in the fridge and use within 2–3 days. Add a little lemon juice and shake to mix just before serving.

Pesto

MAKES ABOUT 250ML
50g pine nuts, toasted
60g basil leaves
3 garlic cloves, peeled and chopped
50g parmesan, freshly grated
125ml olive oil, plus extra to seal
sea salt and black pepper

Whiz the pine nuts, basil, garlic and parmesan in a food processor to a rough paste, stopping to scrape down the sides a few times. With the motor running, slowly trickle in the olive oil. Season to taste with salt and pepper. If not using immediately, transfer to a clean jar and pour a thin layer of olive oil over the surface; this helps to keep the pesto fresh. Seal, refrigerate and use within 5 days.

Tapenade

MAKES ABOUT 275G
40g can anchovy fillets, drained
200g pitted black olives
2 tbsp rinsed and drained capers
1 large garlic clove, peeled and crushed
1 tbsp extra virgin olive oil, plus extra to seal

Whiz the ingredients in a food processor until smooth. Store in a jar or squeezy bottle, topped with a drizzle of olive oil. Chill and use within a week.

Shallot confit

MAKES ABOUT 125G

5 banana shallots, peeled and finely
   chopped
150–200ml olive oil
sea salt and black pepper

In a heavy-based pan, sweat the shallots
with 2–3 tbsp olive oil until beginning to
soften, but not brown. Season well and
add enough olive oil to cover. Cook over
a very low heat for another 30 minutes or
until the shallots are translucent and very
soft. Drain off excess oil before using.

Garlic purée

MAKES ABOUT 180G

5 heads of garlic, cloves separated and
   peeled
25g butter
1 tbsp olive oil, plus extra to seal
100ml vegetable stock (see page 247) or
   water

Gently sauté the garlic cloves with the
butter and olive oil in a small pan for
1–2 minutes until lightly golden. Add the
vegetable stock and lay a crumpled sheet
of baking parchment on top. Simmer
gently for 10–15 minutes until the garlic
is very soft. While it is still hot, transfer
the garlic and half of the cooking fat to a
food processor and purée until smooth.
If the paste is too thick, add a little more
fat and whiz until you have achieved the
required consistency. Cool and store in a
clean squeezy bottle or jar, with a thin
layer of oil on top to prevent it from
turning brown. Chill and use as required.

Celeriac purée

MAKES ABOUT 600G

1 large celeriac (about 500g)
20g butter
sea salt and black pepper
100ml double cream

Peel and chop the celeriac. Melt the
butter in a pan and add the celeriac and
some seasoning. Stir over a high heat for
3–4 minutes until the celeriac is starting
to soften. Reduce the heat, add the cream
and cover the pan with a lid. Cook for
15–20 minutes until the celeriac is very
soft. While still hot, transfer to a food
processor and blend to a fine purée. For a
smoother result, pass the purée through
a fine sieve. Check the seasoning and
reheat before serving.

Turnip purée

MAKES ABOUT 200G

1 large or 2 medium turnips (about 400g)
20g butter
sea salt and black pepper
100ml double cream

Peel the turnips and chop into 1cm dice.
Melt the butter in a pan and add the
turnips. Season and stir over a high heat
for 4–5 minutes until lightly golden.
Lower the heat, add the cream and cover
the pan with a lid. Cook slowly, stirring
occasionally, for 15–20 minutes until the
turnip is very soft. Transfer to a food
processor and whiz to a smooth purée.
For a very smooth purée, pass through a
fine sieve. Adjust the seasoning and
reheat before serving.

Saffron pasta dough

MAKES ABOUT 900G

large pinch of saffron strands
1 tbsp boiling water
500g Italian '00' pasta flour
½ tsp fine sea salt
4 large eggs
6 egg yolks
2 tbsp olive oil

Soak the saffron in 1 tbsp boiling water
for 5 minutes. Sift the flour and salt into
a food processor. Add the eggs, egg yolks
and olive oil. Strain in the saffron water.
Whiz to combine, stopping to scrape
down the sides of the machine twice. The
mixture should form small lumps, which
will hold together as a smooth, firm paste
when pressed with your fingers. Tip onto
a lightly floured surface and knead for a
few minutes until smooth and slightly
springy. Wrap in cling film and leave to
rest for at least 30 minutes before using.

Tomato chutney

MAKES ABOUT 200ML

300g ripe plum tomatoes
2 tbsp extra virgin olive oil
few thyme sprigs
sea salt and black pepper

Put the tomatoes in a heatproof bowl,
pour over boiling water to cover and
leave for 45 seconds to 1 minute to loosen
the skins. Remove and peel off the skins,
then quarter, deseed and finely chop the
flesh. Heat the olive oil in a saucepan and
add the tomatoes, thyme and seasoning.
Cook for 5–7 minutes until the tomatoes
are soft and pulpy, but fairly dry. Remove
the thyme before serving.

Tempura batter

MAKES ABOUT 400ML
125g plain flour
30g cornflour
½ tsp fine sea salt
freshly ground black pepper
150ml chilled sparkling water
150ml chilled beer or light ale

Sift the flour and cornflour together into a large bowl and add the salt and pepper. Using a balloon whisk, quickly whisk in the water and ale. To ensure a light result, do not over-mix; the batter should still be slightly lumpy. Use immediately for coating ingredients before deep-frying.

Crème anglaise

MAKES ABOUT 600ML
250ml whole milk
250ml double cream
75g caster sugar
1 vanilla pod, split
6 large egg yolks

Pour the milk and cream into a heavy-based saucepan and add 1 tbsp sugar. Scrape in the seeds from the vanilla pod and add the pod too. Slowly bring to the boil. Meanwhile, beat the egg yolks and remaining sugar together in a large bowl. As it is about to boil, very slowly pour the creamy milk onto the egg mix, whisking as you do so. Strain through a sieve into a clean pan. Stir the custard over a low heat with a wooden spoon until it has thickened enough to lightly coat the back of the spoon; do not overheat or it will curdle. Strain through a fine sieve into a bowl and leave to cool, stirring from time to time to prevent a skin from forming.

Vanilla ice cream

MAKES ABOUT 1.2 LITRES
500ml whole milk
500ml double cream
200g caster sugar
2 vanilla pods, split (or 2 tsp vanilla extract)
12 large egg yolks

Pour the milk and cream into a heavy-based saucepan and add 2 tbsp sugar. Scrape the seeds from the vanilla pod and add these to the pan with the pod. Slowly bring to the boil. Meanwhile, beat the egg yolks and remaining sugar together in a large bowl. As soon as the creamy milk creeps up the sides of the pan, remove from the heat and gradually pour onto the yolk mix, whisking continuously. Strain the liquid back into the pan. Stir over a low heat with a wooden spoon until the custard thickens enough to lightly coat the back of the spoon. Strain the custard through a fine sieve into a bowl set over another bowl of iced water. Stir the custard occasionally as it cools. Pour the cold custard into an ice cream machine and churn until almost firm. Transfer to a shallow container and freeze until firm. Soften the ice cream at room temperature for 5–10 minutes before serving.

Stock syrup

MAKES ABOUT 500ML
250g sugar
500ml water

Put the sugar and water in a heavy-based saucepan and dissolve over a low heat, then bring to the boil and boil the syrup for 5 minutes. Let cool, then pour into a clean bottle and keep in the fridge for up to 2 weeks. For a reduced stock syrup, boil until reduced by half before cooling.

Dried pear slices

400g caster sugar
400ml water
juice of ½ lemon
3–4 pears

Preheat the oven to its lowest setting and line two baking sheets with silicone liner (silpat or bake-o-glide). Put the sugar, water and lemon juice into a pan and stir over a low heat to dissolve the sugar. Increase the heat and boil for 5 minutes until the syrup is slightly thickened. Leaving the skin on, thinly slice the pears lengthways using a mandolin or sharp knife. (At the restaurant, we use a meat slicer.) As you cut each slice, immediately dip into the syrup then lay on the baking sheet. (We also slice through the centre of each pear to get a pretty slice with the core and stem in place.) The stock syrup can be chilled and re-used for up to a week. Place the pears in the low oven for up to 2 hours until the slices are firm and can be lifted off the silicone easily. If they start to turn brown, prop the oven door open to lower the temperature. Store the cooled pear slices in an airtight container, separated by pieces of baking parchment.

GLOSSARY

ACETATE Thin plastic sheets used to mould desserts in the professional kitchen. Tempered couverture chocolate (see below) is generally spread and cooled on acetate sheets to create different shapes or moulds.

BASTE To spoon or brush pan juices or a marinade over food during cooking to keep it moist and succulent.

BIND To mix liquid or a wet paste into a dry mixture, to bring all the ingredients together.

BLANCH To briefly immerse food in boiling water or hot oil to partially cook it so that the outside is soft while the centre is still crunchy. Often the food is immediately refreshed or plunged into cold water to stop the cooking process and retain colour and texture.

CARAMELISE To cook foods over a high heat until the natural sugars have browned. Also to heat sugar until it dissolves and cooks to a caramel.

CLARIFY To remove solid deposits from food, resulting in a clear liquid. Butter is clarified by melting it and then pouring off the golden oils, often through a muslin-lined sieve. Stock can be clarified by bringing it up to the boil with an egg white mixture, which binds together with the solids, then straining it through a muslin-lined sieve.

CONFIT To cook food slowly, completely submerged in oil or fat, such as melted goose or duck fat, over a low heat. Usually, the food is also stored in the same fat or oil.

COULIS A dessert sauce made from puréed fruit, such as berries or mangoes, mixed with some stock syrup.

COUVERTURE CHOCOLATE A good-quality chocolate containing a minimum of 32% cocoa solids. Mostly used by professional pastry chefs or chocolatiers to coat or mould desserts, it has an excellent flavour and a shiny appearance and thin consistency when melted. Couverture chocolate needs to be tempered (see right) in order to achieve a glossy finish and a hard, crisp texture.

DARIOLE MOULD A small metal mould, about 8cm high, usually with curved sides. The bottom of the mould is narrower than the top. Generally used to make individual servings of desserts or savoury mousses.

DEGLAZE To pour liquid, wine or spirit into a hot pan after it has been used to fry food over a high heat. When stirred, the liquid dislodges any sediment stuck on the bottom of the pan. On boiling, the alcohol evaporates leaving a concentrated flavour in the pan, which enhances the taste of the sauce.

DIGITAL PROBE THERMOMETER A hand-held battery-operated thermometer with a probe attachment, which is used to accurately and instantaneously assess the temperature of solid or liquid food, such as joints of meat or melted chocolate.

FOLD IN To carefully combine a wet or dry ingredient, or a mixture, into a wet mixture by scooping and turning the combined mixtures with a spatula or a large metal spoon in a figure-of-eight motion.

GIANDUJA (OR GIANDUIA) PASTE A thick paste made from chocolate and hazelnut which is often used to make chilled desserts like ice creams and parfaits, as well as chocolate truffles and cakes. Mostly available in commercial quantities from professional or restaurant suppliers.

INFUSE To soak or steep strong flavourings, such as herbs, spices or tea, in hot liquid so that they impart their aromas.

JUS The original French term *au jus* literally means to cook food with its own natural juices. In the culinary world, jus is often used to describe a light meat sauce cooked with additional flavouring such as vegetables, herbs, wine and stock.

LARDING NEEDLE A long needle with a hook or clasp at one end. It is used to secure a long strip of food, such as smoked salmon or bacon, which is then threaded through a thick piece of fish or meat.

LIQUID GLUCOSE A viscous syrup used as a sweetener, which also prevents coarse ice crystals in desserts. Like trimoline (see right), liquid glucose helps to achieve ice creams and sorbets with a smooth, velvety finish. It is available from selected supermarkets.

MACERATE To soak food in liquid or alcohol so it softens and absorbs the flavour of the liquid. Fruit is often soaked in wine, liqueur or stock syrup to tenderise and provide another flavour dimension.

MILLEFEUILLE French term literally meaning 'a thousand layers'. Now widely used to describe dishes with lots of layers.

PINK SALT A preserving salt, also known as *sel rose*, used to retain the vibrant colour of food such as cured meats and foie gras.

POACH To cook food gently by immersing in a liquid such as stock or sugar syrup.

PURÉE To blend or liquefy foods into a smooth paste.

QUENELLE Food shaped into a neat oval using one or two deeply curved spoons to create an attractive presentation.

REDUCE To boil a liquid vigorously until it has evaporated and decreased in volume.

REDUCED STOCK To boil stock until well reduced in volume, leaving a concentrated flavour and a thickened, syrupy consistency. Reduced stock is often used as a glaze for meat dishes.

REFRESH To plunge food into cold water after blanching, to stop the cooking process and preserve the colour and texture.

SCALD To bring a liquid such as milk or cream up to boiling point, just until bubbles begin to appear around the sides of the pan.

SHRED To tear food into small pieces, using two forks moving in opposite directions.

SWEAT To gently fry food with a little oil in a covered pan. The steam in the pan helps to keep the food moist and prevents the food from browning.

TEMPER To take couverture chocolate (see left) through a number of different melting and setting points, which results in changes in the alignment of the molecules in the chocolate during cooling. When set, tempered chocolate has a shiny appearance, breaks in a hard snap and has a smooth 'mouthfeel.'

TRIMOLINE An inverted sugar syrup made from beet or cane sugar, which prevents crystallisation and helps retain moisture in food, keeping it soft and moist. Mostly used in professional kitchens in confectionery, cakes and soft cookies, though we most often add it to ice creams, sorbets and parfaits.

INDEX

ACKNOWLEDGEMENTS

Any restaurant, three-star or not, relies on exceptional people – from the kitchen porter to the sous chef to the wait staff at the front of house. I am very fortunate to be surrounded by such people, many of whom have stuck with me through thick and thin since our early days at the Aubergine.

Take for example, Simone Zanoni, who started off 12 years ago as my kitchen porter at the Aubergine. Simone's infectious energy, tenacity, flair and creativity have quickly taken him through the ranks of the kitchen hierarchy. He trained hard and it makes me proud to see him running the kitchen now. I have no doubt that he will go far in life.

Our kitchen at Royal Hospital Road runs like a well-oiled machine, thanks to my Executive Head Chef, Mark Askew, who has also been working with me since the very beginning. I consider Mark to be one of the most consistent and talented chefs in Britain today.

Providing support to both Mark and Simone is Clare Smyth, an inspirational chef whose technical skills are amazing. She has an articulate palate and a calm and composed manner, which sets her apart from other chefs, particularly in a testosterone-driven, male-dominated industry. Following in Clare's footsteps is Angie Steele, our South African chef who has impressed us with her talent and durability. She will lead the team in our Amsterdam restaurant, due to open soon.

Two other chefs I would like to mention are Sean Burbidge and Paul Walsh, both of whom are extremely focused, disciplined and ambitious. Also thanks to Josh Emett who heads up our restaurant in New York, and Nicolas Defremont who takes care of the dining room there.

If you've ever met the man, you would remember Jean-Claude Breton. One thing for sure, he remembers you. As our top *maître d*, not only is Jean-Claude incredibly professional, he makes it his mission to remember every guest's name as well as what they had for dinner. Who needs a computer when you've got a memory like Jean-Claude's? As far as I'm concerned, the man could run MI5.

Our three stars would merely be an aspiration if it were not for the phenomenal support we get from our operations and reservations teams. Without the likes of Gillian Thomson and Nicola Monks, we would not be able to focus our attention on cooking and serving fantastic food.

Special thanks to everyone involved in the production of this book: Tony Turnbull, my editor at the Times who has acquired so much food knowledge he could open a restaurant of his own; Mark Sargeant (or 'Sarge' as he is affectionately called), my right hand man who understands me so well; Emily Quah, the 'yummy mummy' of the year, whose reliability, dedication and aptitude is admirable; Janet Illsley for her remarkable efficiency, commitment and attention to detail; Helen Lewis and Quentin Bacon for making the book look absolutely gorgeous; and to Anne Furniss and Alison Cathie for their support and confidence in this personal endeavour.

Eternal thanks to Chris Hutcheson who makes everything possible, and my extended gratitude to Jo Barnes who patiently manages my PR. And last but not least, thanks to Tana, Megan, Jack, Holly and Matilda for always being there for me.

EDITORIAL DIRECTOR *Anne Furniss*
CREATIVE DIRECTOR *Helen Lewis*
PROJECT EDITOR *Janet Illsley*
TEXT: THE 3-STAR EXPERIENCE *Tony Turnbull*
RECIPE RESEARCH AND TESTING *Emily Quah,*
    assisted by Cathryn Evans
PHOTOGRAPHER *Quentin Bacon*
FOOD STYLISTS *Simone Zanoni, Mark Sargeant*
PRODUCTION *Ruth Deary, Vincent Smith*

This edition first published in 2008 by
Quadrille Publishing Limited
Alhambra House
27–31 Charing Cross Road
London WC2H 0LS
www.quadrille.co.uk

Text © 2007 Gordon Ramsay
Photography © 2007 Quentin Bacon
Design and layout © 2007 Quadrille Publishing
Limited

Cataloguing in Publication Data: a catalogue record
for this book is available from the British Library.

ISBN: 978 184400 659 5

Printed in China

Notes

• The three-star recipes in this book, as photographed, originate from Gordon Ramsay, Royal Hospital Road. They have been adapted and carefully tested for the domestic kitchen. Nevertheless, many of the recipes are still challenging and demand skill and precision on the part of the home cook.
• It is absolutely essential to use good-quality ingredients in prime condition.
• All spoon measures are level unless otherwise stated: 1 tsp = 5ml spoon; 1 tbsp = 15ml spoon.
• All herbs are fresh, and all pepper is freshly ground black pepper unless otherwise suggested.
• It is recommended that free-range eggs are used. Anyone who is pregnant or in a vulnerable health group should avoid those recipes that contain raw egg whites or lightly cooked eggs.
• Timings are provided as guidelines, with a description of colour or texture where appropriate, but the reader must rely on their own judgement as to when a dish is properly cooked. The oven timings apply to fan-assisted ovens. If using a conventional oven, increase the temperature by 15°C (1 Gas Mark). Use an oven thermometer to check the accuracy of your oven.